ABOUT

Piper Bayard is an author and a recovering attorney. She is also a belly dancer, a mom, and a former hospice volunteer. She currently pens spy thrillers with Jay Holmes, as well as her own post-apocalyptic science fiction.

Jay Holmes is a forty-five year veteran of field intelligence operations spanning from the Cold War fight against the Soviets, the East Germans, and the terrorist organizations they sponsored to the present Global War on Terror. Piper is the public face of their partnership.

Together, Bayard & Holmes author nonfiction articles and books on espionage and foreign affairs, as well as fictional spy thrillers. They are the bestselling authors of *The Spy Bride* from the Risky Brides Bestsellers Collection and *Spycraft: Essentials.*

When they aren't writing or, in Jay's case, busy with "other work," Piper and Jay are enjoying their families, hiking, exploring, talking foreign affairs, laughing at their own rude jokes, and questing for the perfect chocolate cake recipe. If you think you have that recipe, please share it with them at their email below.

To receive notices of upcoming Bayard & Holmes releases, subscribe to the Bayard & Holmes Covert Briefing. You can contact Bayard & Holmes at their website BayardandHolmes.com, at @piperbayard on Twitter, or at their email, BayardandHolmes@protonmail.com.

ALSO BY BAYARD & HOLMES

NONFICTION

Spycraft: Essentials

Key Figures in Espionage

Key Moments in Espionage

Spycraft Series Coming Soon

Key People & Wars

———

FICTION BY BAYARD & HOLMES

The Spy Bride

Apex Predator Series Coming Soon

The Panther of Baracoa

The Leopard of Cairo

The Caiman of Iquitos

———

FICTION BY PIPER BAYARD

Firelands

TIMELINE IRAN

STONE AGE TO NUCLEAR AGE

BAYARD & HOLMES

Shoe Phone Press
2770 Arapahoe Road #132-229
Lafayette, CO 80026

To the brave and determined people of Iran ...

May you one day be free.

CONTENTS

INTRODUCTION

One of the critical international issues on the minds of West-erners today is the question of Iranian atomic capabilities. Is Iran developing nuclear weapons? If so, should we do something to stop it? Who is "we," and precisely what would that "something" be? How much would that "something" cost, and to whom?

All of these questions are worth considering. To consider them rationally, we need to know who the Iranians are, and what underlying agendas they have. What do they want, and how much are they willing to pay for it?

It's easy to be confused by what we see and by what the Iranians say. When Iranian protests range from "Death to America" to "Death to the clerics," it's difficult to get an accurate impression of who comprises the Iranian government, and what Iranians might actually be like or think about that government.

Long before the poorly-educated, megalomaniac Ayatollah Khomeini returned to Iran to drag it back into an eighth century style of government, there was a developing nation called Iran. Long before there was a nation called Iran, there was an empire called Persia. The history that took Iran from the Stone Age to a modern nation is worth considering when wondering what today's Iranians think about the events occurring in their country.

When it comes to history, we find it helpful to use a timeline for understanding the cultural journey and development of a nation. The timeline we have compiled in this booklet is by no means extensive. That would be an encyclopedia. Our goal was to hit the highlights and give readers a brief, digestible overview of the history of the country we know as Iran, as well as a feel for the political development of that country from a haven for Neanderthals through thousands of years of monarchy to the current Islamic fundamentalist theocracy.

And who are we to write this book? Piper is an author and a recovering attorney who has worked daily with Holmes for the past decade, learning about foreign affairs, espionage history, and field techniques for the purpose of writing both fiction and nonfiction. Holmes is a forty-five-year veteran of the Intelligence Community. Since Holmes is covert, Piper is the public face of their partnership.

Come walk with us now through the brilliant kaleidoscope that is Iran's past as we attempt to understand what lies ahead.

STONE AGE TO NEBUCHADNEZZAR I

c. 800,000 BC

Neanderthals inhabited the Kashafrud Basin in Khorasan, now northeastern Iran, as evidenced by stone tools made from quartz that were dated by archaeologist C. Thibault. The National Museum of Iran agreed with the dating.

100,000 BC – 60,000 BC

Neanderthals inhabited Shanidar Cave in what is today an area of modern Iraq, according to skeletal remains found by archeologists.

Archeologists also located Neolithic tools in at least three distinct major sites in modern Iran. The dating of the tools remains somewhat controversial, and estimates range from between sixty thousand and one hundred thousand years old.

15,000 BC

There might have been someone in ancient Persia, and they might have been drinking wine.

Some archaeologists claim a wine vase from 15,000 BC was unearthed in Iran, but multiple well-respected scientific sources have been unable to verify that. That doesn't mean it isn't true. It means there is only so much time we're willing to spend trying to verify one artifact.

9000 BC

Humans inhabited ancient Persia.

For simplicity's sake, we define "ancient Persia" as being the land between the Caspian Sea, the Indus river, the Euphrates River, and the current Iranian coast.

Human artifacts, including jewelry, refined pottery, and metal tools, have been found in this area that date back to 9000 BC. The quality of these artifacts indicates that nearly eleven thousand years before Paul Revere smithed silver tea sets, skilled artisans in ancient Persia created intricate, sophisticated works.

7200 BC

Villagers in Choga Bonut, western Persia, farmed and crafted high-quality clay pottery.

7000 BC

There were definitely people inhabiting the Zagros Mountains of Iran, and they were definitely drinking wine.

Wine vases from the Zagros Mountains date from 7000 BC, proving that, although black market English, Canadian, and American whiskey now enters Iran via small boats every night, booze has been there for a long time.

Archaeologists also found Neolithic evidence at a place that would later become the busy trade center of Susa, and that Iranians today call Shush.

6800 BC

Villagers in Choga Mish, near Choga Bonut, inhabited a regional trade center and practiced agriculture. They left behind rich evidence that was being explored at the time of the twentieth century Iranian Islamic Revolution. The "revolutionaries" felt threatened by science and saw the practice of archaeology as a heresy, so they destroyed the dig site and stole the artifacts. Fortunately, work from the dig site was published prior to 1979.

5000 BC

Someone in Susa was making painted pottery.

4000 BC - 3000 BC

According to early Bronze Age sites, the Jiroft agricultural civilization irrigated their crops and produced sophisticated jewelry and metal tools during this period. They were also involved in East-West trade.

3100 BC – 2900 BC

People in the region used clay tablets with Sumerian Cuneiform writing. The earliest dates of these tablets are still debated in Iran, but they co-date the Mesopotamian city-building activity in Iraq and on the fringes of Iran.

For comparison, during the same period, the Brits were building Stonehenge, and in North America, Cochise people were just beginning to cultivate corn, but not squash and beans. The Egyptians were building large cities and monuments.

2700 BC

The Elamites, a non-Semitic people, established a kingdom in western Persia with Susa as its capital. They introduced complex government with power shared by three family members and regional authority relegated to under-lords. A central system controlled trade, and regions were tasked with producing the products that were best suited to their natural resources and local talents.

This inter-regional economy was quite productive and supported a higher standard of living for people within the kingdom. The Elamites preferred trade with surrounding countries while maintaining well-organized military forces that could resist invasion by powerful neighbors in Mesopotamia.

Some anthropologists claim this culture had a written language, but recognized experts in early languages agree that the evidence is fake. Those ancient people may not have written, but they had a well-established civilization.

2000 BC

Unable to find their Dungeons & Dragons dice, the people of ancient Persia invented chess.

1764 BC

Hammurabi of Babylonia conquered most of the Elamite kingdom. The Elamites survived in the mountains beyond Hammurabi's reach.

c. 1730 BC

The Elamites dealt a devastating defeat to the armies of Hammurabi's son, Samsuiluna, and regained their kingdom. Western Persia entered a period of two hundred years of comparative isolation from the outside world.

1500 BC - 1250 BC

The Anzanite faction of the Elamites established a strong dynasty, and the Elamite Empire grew toward Mesopotamia and what had become a strong Assyrian Empire.

1208 BC

Assyrian King Tukulti-Ninurta died, and Assyria fell into internal strife over succession to the throne. The Elamites seized the opportunity and campaigned against the Assyrian armies. They captured Babylon and took the famous Hammurabi Stela containing the inscribed Code of Hammurabi to Susa.

c. 1150 BC

Nebuchadnezzar I united northern and central Babylon, an area we call modern Iraq. He attacked and defeated the Elamite Empire. Again, the Elamites retreated to mountainous areas and survived.

2

PERSIAN ROOTS TO PERSIAN TRIUMPH

c. 1000 BC

The struggle between Babylonian kingdoms and the Elamites continued, but it created an opportunity for outsiders. Fierce nomadic horsemen entered the Persian plains from the north. They spoke a language that is believed to be the root language for modern Persian. They were highly mobile and avoided direct confrontations with large armies from Babylon and from what remained of Elam.

The largest and most organized of the invading nomads were known as the Medes. They formed the foundation of what would become a strong military group that lent strength to a Persian expansion.

c. Who-Knows-When BC

Somewhere between 6000 BC and 100 BC, a man known in the West as Zoroaster founded what most historians believe to be the first organized, monotheist religion to survive to modern times.

Zoroastrian religion states that Ahura Mazda, a.k.a. God, is benevolent and compassionate. Man may only enter the kingdom of heaven through acts of compassion and kindness. It is a religion that preaches cooperation and free thought. According to Zoroaster, all people have and should embrace free will. Based on available historical literature, the religion has roots as far back as 1800 BC. Zoroastrianism had a strong developmental influence on Persian civilization and economy.

612 BC

The Babylonians helped the Medes capture the Assyrian center of Nineveh, a city in the north of modern Iraq. The Assyrian Empire collapsed.

c. 600 BC

The now-settled Median people formed an alliance state with Babylonia, Lydia, and Egypt. The great federation allowed for more-organized trade and agriculture. Arts flourished across the region. Wealth increased.

c. 590 BC

Cyrus the Great was born in Anshan, Iran. In Persia he was known as Kurus. He grew up to change the course of South Asian history.

c. 559 BC

Cyrus ascended the Achaemenid throne and ruled under the over-lordship of the powerful Medians.

553 BC

Cyrus raised a revolt against the Median overlords. He used remarkable diplomatic skill and inspired various tribes from fringe areas to join him.

549 BC

Cyrus's army defeated the city of Ecbatana and completed his conquest of the Medians. He was wise and magnanimous in conquest. He co-opted many of the most popular and proficient Medians and allowed them local rule under his over-lordship. Cyrus allowed local religions and customs to continue unmolested.

547 BC

Thanks to good, but unusual, advice from his general, Harpagus, Cyrus defeated Lydia at the battle of Tymbra. With the wind at his back, he placed his malodorous dromedaries in the front of his main army to lead the charge against Lydian cavalry. The Lydian horses had never been near dromedaries before. The horses panicked, and the Lydian cavalry were defeated.

546 BC

Before defenses could be organized, Cyrus moved quickly against Lydian strongholds, and he defeated Lydia decisively by the end of the year.

540 BC

Cyrus ordered his laborers to dig a canal to lower ground from the Euphrates River, which was a natural protective barrier for the east side of the otherwise walled city of Babylon. The water receded to a passable level, and Cyrus's troops entered Babylon by crossing the river. They forced the surrender of the Babylonian garrison.

Two thousand, three hundred years later, General Sherman remembered Cyrus's achievement and attempted to use the Mississippi River to form canals that allowed the flanking of Vicksburg, Mississippi from beyond the range of her guns above the cliffs, but that is a story for another day.

530 BC

Cyrus the Great died in battle in central Asia. His son, Cambyses II, took his place.

525 BC

Persia conquered Egypt.

521 BC

The Royal Spear Bearer Darius became the Emperor Darius I and married both the widow of Cambyses and the daughter of Cyrus.

Darius put down internal revolts using diplomatic skills and decisive military actions. He wisely divided the kingdom into regions to be governed by local kings that he selected and which served under his over-lordship.

518 BC

Darius founded Persepolis as a new capital of Persia.

He controlled court politics in a city of his own design and with a population that he selected. He had canals built to connect the Red Sea to the Nile River and coined a universal currency of standard measure for the Empire, which further promoted trade and a growing economy. A renaissance in architecture spread across the Persian Empire.

517 BC

Darius conquered the Punjab area of India. He used advanced chariot tactics to extend Persian rule further into Libya.

Trade flourished across the empire. Local customs were tolerated. The people under Persian rule enjoyed a higher standard of living and more rights than most of them had known under their previous rulers.

512 BC

The armies of Darius I reached the lower Danube River in modern Bulgaria. This marked the greatest limit of expansion for the great Persian Empire.

490 BC

Persia attacked Greece, but the invasion failed.

486 BC

Darius I died and Xerxes took the throne. Xerxes outsourced his engineering needs by searching for foreign architects to add to the diversity and development of Persian architecture.

481 BC

Persia invaded Greece again. After a delaying action by a small Spartan force at the narrow pass at Thermopylae, the Persians reached Athens and sacked the Parthenon.

Small, maneuverable Greek naval vessels defeated reinforcing Persian amphibious forces at the Battle of Salamis. The Persian invaders retreated as the Greeks organized more resistance.

Two thousand, four hundred years later, a young American naval genius from Boulder, Colorado, named Arleigh Burke devised tactics based on the lessons of that ancient battle along with the land tactics of the Greeks. Those tactics allowed him to gain naval victories against far-superior Japanese forces in the waters north of Guadalcanal in 1943.

332 BC

Alexander III of Macedonia, a.k.a. Alexander the Great, conquered Egypt and Persia. The city of Persepolis was destroyed on Alexander's orders. When touring the ruins, he was filled with regret for the destruction of the magnificent city.

312 BC

A committee of some of Alexander's generals set up the Seleucid Dynasty to rule Persia.

247 BC – 224 BC

The Parthians of northwest Persia rose up, and by using something of a "throw the foreigners out" propaganda campaign and concentrating their forces at strategic locations for quick offenses, they defeated the Seleucid Dynasty. The Parthians introduced advanced horse breeding and developed horses that were capable of carrying fast, armored archers.

Painting reached new heights in Persia, and Persian artists produced highly representative and remarkably detailed paintings of historical events.

36 BC

A Parthian army took advantage of its expert mounted archers and defeated Mark Anthony of Rome in Azerbaijan.

A young American tank commander by the name of George Patton, as well as German armored tactician Hans Guderian, studied this battle and used its lessons to great effect in WWII.

208 AD – 224 AD

The Sassanians, elite members of Parthian society who were trained for military service and prominent government office, took over what is modern day Iran. They developed a highly-organized military system with specialist reservists backing up elite, well-trained units.

This system relied on rapid communication via messengers, mirror messages, and trumpet calls to mobilize in time to meet threats from foreign armies. At the same time, it allowed for the maintenance of a large, professional army, without paying salaries to reservists except during times of training or war. These trained reservists were able to use their engineering skills in their local communities to promote the building of roads, bridges, agricultural canals etc.

Under the Sassanians, art continued to progress. They developed the vaulted dome, which became a symbol of Islamic culture.

450 AD - 484 AD

Huns from central Asia repeatedly attacked Sassanian towns and sometimes cities. The Huns used fast, light cavalry tactics and never remained in one place long enough for an army to form up and challenge them.

570 AD

Mohammad was born in Arabia. He founded the Islamic religion. At about the same time, the oldest known surviving Persian carpet was produced in Iran.

590 AD

Persian King Khosrow II revived the Sassanid Empire with westward campaigns into Byzantium.

612 AD

Khosrow II captured Jerusalem.

619 AD

Khosrow II reached Alexandria, Egypt. This signified the last high water mark of the great Persian Empires.

636 AD

At the Battle of the Qadisiya, on the banks of the Euphrates River, Islamic Arab invaders defeated Persian General Rustam and his soldiers. This signified the beginning of the end of the last great Persian Empire.

3

ISLAMIC ARAB INVASION

642 AD

At the battle of Nahavand, an invading army of thirty thousand Arabs defeated a larger Persian army led by General Mardan Shah. Mardan allowed his army to pursue a band of a few thousand Arabs into mountain passes, where well-armed Arabs holding the surrounding high ground ambushed them. The Persians suffered about twenty thousand deaths, and the remainder were wounded or routed.

The Arabs entered the high Persian plains and sacked several cities before the Persians could reorganize. Emperor Yazdgerd III retreated to the city of Merv, and with help from the Huns and Turks, he held off the Arabs for a few years. Yazdgerd traveled further east into Persia, but his own governors were in revolt. He was unable to organize a resistance against the Islamic invaders.

652 AD

The Persian Emperor Yasdgerd III was assassinated in Merv by an inconspicuous local miller who was able to approach him without alerting his guards.

Yasdgerd's son, Pirooz II, did his best to save the Sassanid Empire from the Rashidun Caliphate, and then the Umayyad Caliphate, but he was unable to bring together enough Persian warlords. Pirooz II eventually fled to China, where he died. This left the once-great Persian Empire subjected to the rule of the Umayyad Caliphate.

656 AD

Ali ibn Abi Talid, the son-in-law of Muhammad, was installed as the Caliph in Kufa near Basra and ruled the Umayyad Empire, which included much of Persia.

661 AD

Ali was assassinated in the mosque in Kufa. Differing opinions over the holy status of Ali at this time created the Islamic schism between what are now "Shia" and "Sunni" Muslims.

680 AD

Hussein, son of Ali, was defeated by the Umayyad Army in Karbala. This solidified the split between Shia and Sunni Muslims.

750 AD

The Abbasid clan, descendants of Muhammad's Uncle Abbas, decided they were the rightful heirs to Muhammad's authority, and they formed an army that defeated the Umayyad army, taking control of most of the Umayyad Caliphate. They moved the capitol to Baghdad.

817 AD

The compassionate and learned Eighth Imam Ali ar Ridha foretold his own murder and instructed his servants on his burial. Fighting between Arabs and Persians broke out across the Caliphate.

945 AD

Uyid warriors, who were Shias, marched into Baghdad and defeated the Caliph's forces. They established a capitol at Qom.

900 - 1000 AD

Persia re-established strong East-West trade, and Persian culture flourished once more. A strong currency based on standard measures was re-instituted in the empire.

1006 AD

In the Persian city of Gonbad-e Qabus Amir, Shams Qabus ibn Voshmgir, ruler of the Ziyarid Dynasty, had a tower constructed of baked brick. Some sources believe it was meant to be a tomb, though no corpses have been found in it. Others speculate that it was built as an observatory. With a height of approximately 170 ft (52 meters), it is still reputed to be the tallest solid brick structure ever built. The ratio of the height to the diameter is Pi.

1020 AD

Fast, mobile warriors from what we now call Turkestan invaded Persia. They were fierce and merciless. They unwittingly repeated military events from Persia's history by defeating the more-settled and sedentary Persians of the Caliphate.

In this sense, the history of Iran resembles that of the British Isles. Barbaric people took well developed areas from more-settled and civilized people. They, in turn, became more civilized, only to be invaded by another wave of more-barbaric people, and so the cycle continues.

1038 AD

Turkish Seljuk warriors invaded Persia in force and defeated a Persian army in battle near Merv. They decided to dismount long enough to stay and build a city, establishing a capitol in Isfahan.

1048 AD

Persian mathematician, philosopher, and poet Omar Khayyam was born. He was a great linguist, and he translated significant works from around the world into Farsi. He also wrote his own important works on algebra and geometry. His poetry and philosophy had a long-lasting impact both inside and outside Iran.

1055 AD

The apparently romantically-inclined Seljuk people had multiplied. They invaded Mesopotamia and established a capitol in Baghdad. They, too, began absorbing the well-developed science and methods of government and commerce from Persia and Mesopotamia.

1118 AD

The great Seljuk leader Muhammad Ibn Malik Shah died. There was no succession in place, and the Seljuk Empire broke up into smaller kingdoms across Mesopotamia and Persia.

1221 AD

Fierce, fast-riding warlord Genghis Khan and his massive army descended from the northeast during their stroll from Mongolia. They liked taking anything they found. They didn't like taking no for an answer. They conquered as they went with rapid successes and few delays.

The cities of Khorasan, Persia, calculated that they outnumbered Genghis's army four-to-one and refused to surrender. While it's true they outnumbered the invaders, the Persians were spread out in garrisons and were not as swift as the Mongols. Genghis was insulted by the Persians' failure to surrender, so he captured the cities one by one and ordered everyone in them to be beheaded.

Genghis and his sons are not remembered fondly in the Islamic world.

1258 AD

The Mongols, led by Genghis's grandson Hogul, conquered most of Persia, Mesopotamia, and Syria. They crushed the Caliphate of Baghdad and killed eight hundred thousand people in the process. The area fell under the rule of the great Mongolian/Chinese Khanate.

Persian society did not attain pre-Mongol levels of sophistication again until the twentieth century.

1348 AD

Tamerlane, a descendant of Mongols, stylized himself in the fashion of Genghis Khan. He captured what remained of eastern Persia and set up another rule. He was no great rider of the plains, but his soldiers were great riders, and he was a good organizer and a skilled political animal. He became a menace to all Islamic areas by raiding Islamic areas of India and Islamic communities further west.

1405 AD

The Islamic Timurid Dynasty was formed in Persia. Arts flourished anew. Once again, Persian miniature painting techniques were perfected.

1406 AD

The Shi'ite Muslim, Turkic-speaking Kara Koyunlu Dynasty, a.k.a. Black Sheep Turkomans, moved its capital to Tabriz.

1469 AD

The Sunni Muslim, Turkic-speaking Aq Qoyunlu Dynasty, a.k.a. the White Sheep Turkomans, took control of most of Persia.

1501 AD

Life turned grim again in Persia as it fell into a new dark age of ignorance and suffering. A Shia Islamic warlord and religious zealot of questionable religious qualifications by the name of Shah Ismail began a reconquest of Persia. He was an effective warrior, if a savage one, and he preached slaughter and torture of all that was not Shia.

Within eight years Shah Ismail conquered most of what is now modern day Iran and established the Safavid Dynasty. He made Shia Islam the state religion, and anything other than Shia was punishable by death. He installed loyal followers to control religious authority in Persia. He was not the last barbaric politician to employ religious-based hatred in order to control Persia.

1588 AD

Shah Abbas I ascended the Safavid throne in Persia. He was far less ignorant and ruthless than Shah Ismail. Persia began rebuilding a civilization, and for a century, literacy, science, and arts flourished once more. Architecture returned to great heights in Persia with the building of impressive arched bridges. Canals and irrigation were reformed. Engineering skills, literature, and art returned to the forefront of life in Persia. Abbas did not rock the religious boat. He reaffirmed Shia domination, but he installed his own selected "religious authorities."

4

FROM RENAISSANCE TO OIL

1650 AD

The magnificent Khaju Bridge of twenty-four arches was built over the Isfahan River during the reign of Shah Abbas II.

While a new age of art, literature, architecture, and engineering flourished in Persia, the question of dynastic successions left it in a weakened condition politically. In the last half of the seventeenth century and the beginning of the eighteenth century, many of Persia's politically elite focused too much on internal rivalries and failed to deal effectively with foreign relations.

1722 AD

A charismatic Afghan chieftain by the name of Mahmud Ghilzai Khan revolted against his Persian overlords and overcame tribal enmities to form a united army. He invaded and captured Isfahan and ruled much of eastern Persia.

1725 AD

In a move that would make George R. R. Martin proud, Mahmud Khan invited the leading citizens of Isfahan to a feast and slaughtered them. After that adventure in indigestion, Mahmud Khan's confidant, who was also his cousin, murdered him.

1729 AD

Persian General Nadir Qoli defeated and evicted Afghan invaders from eastern Persia on behalf of the Safavid Dynasty.

Nadir is sometimes described as "the Napoleon of Persia." Born Nadir Qoli Beg of the Turkish Afshar tribe, his life began in poverty and soon went downhill from there when he and his mother were captured into slavery by the Ozbegs. Nadir escaped the Ozbegs and found his calling as a soldier with his tribe, the Turkish Afshar of the Khorasan region of Persia.

He quickly rose in the ranks of the Afshar, but then he fell out of favor with their leader. Nadir fought with the Afghans for a while until he fell out with them, as well.

Having burned his bridges, Nadir moved on and offered his services to the Safavid Dynasty to fight against the Afghans, driving them out of Khorasan and slaughtering thousands of the citizens of Isfahan.

Tamasp II was crowned Shah of the Safavid Dynasty.

1732 AD

While Nadir was distracted with an uprising in Isfahan, Tamasp II moved against the Turks and lost Georgia and Armenia to them. More than a little annoyed, Nadir deposed Tamasp II and placed the infant Abbas III on the Safavid throne with himself as regent. No one really thought that Abbas III was in charge.

1735 AD

Yet another foreign force invaded Persia. This time, it was a well-equipped Turkish army that entered western Persia. Nadir solidified his political position with the Safavids by defeating and evicting the Turks.

1736 AD

Nadir, tired of pretending the child Shah Abbas III was any kind of ruler, deposed that last member of the Safavid Dynasty and declared himself Nadir Shah Afshar, establishing the Afsharid Dynasty. According to Nadir Shah's French Jesuit physician, Nadir Shah was indifferent to religion and had none of his own. He did, however, occasionally pretend to be nominally more Islamic than the Pope. Nadir Shah attempted throughout his reign to reconcile the Sunnis and the Shi'ites within the Persian Empire since his armies were comprised of both, but to no avail.

1739 AD

Nadir Shah invaded and defeated Afghanistan. He then invaded India and sacked Delhi, reportedly slaughtering thirty thousand of its residents. He plundered fortunes in jewels from the Mughal Empire, including the famous Koh-i-noor diamond and the Golden Peacock Throne, and shipped them to Persia.

1740 AD

The Astrakhanid Dynasty of Uzbekistan and Turkistan collapsed. Nadir Shah quickly conquered the region and incorporated it into Persia.

1743 AD

Nadir Shah built Persia's first navy and took it out for a spin to conquer Bahrain and Oman.

1747 AD

Nadir Shah became increasingly brutal over the years and was known for torturing, maiming, and killing his own people.

Finally, enough was enough. Nadir's bodyguards assassinated him.

Nadir's loyal bodyguard commander, Ahmad Shah Durrani, immediately nicked Nadir Shah's royal seal from his dead finger and the Koh-i-noor diamond from his dead arm, and high-tailed it to Kandahar. Once there, Durrani declared himself the Shah of Afghanistan, and he is considered the "Father of Afghanistan" to this day.

Many of the strongest leaders that could have risen to rule a united empire were long since dead, thanks to the cruel hand of Nadir Shah, and the vast Persian Empire of the Afsharid Dynasty fell into civil war along predominantly ethnic divisions.

1750 AD

Karim Khan managed to rise through the mayhem of the civil war and establish the Zand Dynasty. Karim attempted to solidify control by killing off various ethnic and political groups. His genocidal campaign was not completely successful.

1794 AD

Agha Muhammad Khan, a survivor of Karim's brutality in his youth, led an army against Karim and decisively defeated the Zand Dynasty. He reunited much of the Persian Empire under the Kadjar Dynasty.

1796 AD

Agha Muhammad's servants assassinated him.

1798 AD

Fath Ali Shah rose to the top of the Persian political heap. He reinvigorated East-West trade, and Persia entered a new age of prosperity.

1813 AD

Not all Azerbaijanis liked being Persian. In the northern reaches of Azerbaijan, they joined the Russians and Armenians to invade Azerbaijan. They defeated the Persian garrisons, and Fath Ali Shah signed a treaty ceding Persia's northern territories to the Russia Empire, including what is now Georgia, Dagestan, most of Azerbaijan, and northern Armenia.

1823 AD

Fath Ali Shah wisely signed a peace treaty with the Turks that defined their mutual border.

1828 AD

Persia lost another war with the Russian Empire and ceded control of the Caucasus and the north Caspian shore to Russia, including the rest of modern-day Azerbaijan and Armenia.

1879 AD

Great Britain invaded Afghanistan from British India, and at a high cost in men and material, it defeated the Afghan tribes. Within weeks, the British troops started wondering why they came to Afghanistan. The invasion indirectly pitted the Russian Empire against Great Britain.

The Persians laughed.

1881 AD

The Russian Empire ignored the British Empire long enough to invade and capture Turkmenistan from Persia.

The Russians laughed, and the British remained silent on the point, as they were busy in India and elsewhere.

The sentiments of the Turkmenistan peasants were not recorded.

1890 AD

Persians embraced comic political opera and elevated it to an art form within one hundred, twenty years. Persian leader Naser al-Din Shah Kadjar infuriated the Persian people by selling tobacco-growing concessions to European companies. Those concessions seemed like easy money to the Shah and required no capital investment.

1891 AD

Persian mullahs issued a "fatwa," which is a holy war declaration, against anyone cooperating with the European tobacco concessions.

1896 AD

Naser al-Din Shah was murdered in a mosque. It seemed like easy money to the mullahs and required no capital investment by them.

1900 AD

Persia granted mineral rights to Great Britain. It seemed like easy money to the Persian monarchy and required no capital investment by Persia.

1906 AD

The mullahs instigated anti-European riots. About fifteen thousand Brits took refuge in the British Embassy property. The tea schedule was disrupted. It seemed like easy money to the mullahs. It cost them no capital investment.

To the mullahs' dismay, a constitutional movement led by educated Persians took over the riots. Mozzafar ad-Din Shah agreed to a constitution that limited his power.

While their ancestors were fierce warriors who ruled with iron fists, the Persian throne now seemed to be at the mercy of multiple factions, both foreign and domestic. Alliances that keep the throne intact depended on the political wind of the day.

To the dismay of the mullahs, Persia held elections for a democratic parliament. If the monarchy was something the mullahs hated, democracy was something they loathed and feared.

1907 AD

Russia's beleaguered monarchy and the far-stretched British conferred with their respective accountants and divided up Iran between them into spheres of influence.

1908 AD

Russian troops put down a rebellion directed by the mullahs, and Great Britain drilled the first Middle Eastern oil well.

———

Let the fun begin.

———

5

THE ASCENSION OF MOHAMMAD REZA SHAH PAHLAVI

THE BIRTH OF THE MIDDLE EASTERN OIL INDUSTRY USHERED IN ONE of the most critical, most frequently-twisted, and most frequently-misunderstood or ignored periods in the formation of modern Iran.

1911 AD

The elected Persian parliament, the Majlis, appointed a brilliant American lawyer and financier, William Morgan Shuster, to the post of Treasurer General. The Majlis trusted him because he helped them for several years with his expertise, political connections, and financial support from his personal wealth as they attempted to form a constitution for Persia. Shuster operated on the belief that a stable Nationalist "pro-Persian" government in Persia would be better for Persia and for any potential trade partners, including the United States.

Shuster imported a team of American banking experts and white collar crime specialists and began implementing reforms to reduce corruption and build a treasury. Shuster's efforts boded well for the future of a constitutional and democratic society in

Persia. Naturally, he was unpopular with British oil developers, Russian Czarists, and their Persian lackeys who grew wealthy from the foreign intervention.

Great Britain used skilled diplomatic pressure on Iran to attempt to oust Shuster. Russia used standard Russian-style diplomacy and dispatched an army of twelve thousand well-equipped soldiers to invade Persia. The Russians provided muscle for the installation of an obese twelve-year-old named Sultan Ahmed Shah. Russian artillery shelled the Majlis and destroyed it.

Democratic Nationalism died an agonizing death across Persia. In later decades, Iran's politically ambitious religious fanatics would rail against the filthy Western devils for the invasion, but at the time, many of the religious fanatics cooperated with the British and the Russians in the hope of destroying democracy in Persia.

Neither the United Kingdom nor Russia wanted to drag the US government and its idealistic views into Persia, so killing Shuster and his team would have been a political disaster for the United Kingdom. Shuster and his Americans departed Persia with their lives intact, due to British maneuvering. The British Foreign Office, with the skilled help of MI-6 and the Royal Navy, and without public disclosures to the voters in the United Kingdom, managed to shape the resultant fallout to their advantage, and the UK gained control of southern Iran and its oil fields.

A great opportunity for freedom and democracy in Persia was lost. Shuster later published a book, *The Strangling of Persia*, which was highly critical of the United Kingdom and Russia.

1913 AD

Thanks in large part to the United Kingdom's strong grip on Persian oil reserves, the already pre-eminent Royal Navy took an important technological leap in naval warfare and converted its fleet from coal to oil. The advantages were tremendous. They were able to drive more heavily-armored ships at higher speeds, thanks to the efficiency of oil-fired boilers. The Royal Navy gained even more mobility because the ships required less frequent refueling.

For comparison, the US Navy began the conversion to oil in 1908 with tests on land-based boilers and machinery mock ups. The United States committed to the conversion based purely on science rather than on economics because it had a reliable domestic supply of oil.

July 28, 1914 AD

Austria made one of the most asinine political decisions in human history. Backed by assurances from the ever-confident and never bright Kaiser Wilhelm of Germany, Austria invaded Serbia. It seemed like a great decision to the apparently intellectually-challenged Austrian royalty and their ill-trained military leaders. It required little capital investment the first week, and victory should have been quick and profitable. The "easy one month victory" turned into the great human tragedy of WWI.

Persia had no idea which way to turn; therefore, it made no turns and declared neutrality. It seemed like a great idea and required no capital investment. However, the neutrality worked about as well as any neutral declaration does when it's not backed up by military capacity. The Ottomans wanted Persian oil. The British intended to keep it. The "neutral" Persia became one more bloody battlefield in the chaos of WWI. The Persian economy was disrupted, agriculture suffered, and children went hungry.

1919 AD

Having successfully defended its hold on Afghanistan through WWI, the British government asked itself why it was in Afghanistan. The answer was two-fold. One reason was that the

British presence in Afghanistan was a response to raids into British-controlled India by swift Afghan mounted warriors. The second, more critical reason was simply to keep the Russians out.

Then it occurred to the British Foreign Office that the cruelest thing they could do to the annoying communist Soviet Union was to leave it to tangle with Afghanistan. The British withdrew their troops from the profitless Afghan territory and reinforced their border between Afghanistan and India.

Note: If you glance at a map, remember that what is now Pakistan was then part of India.

Persian Prime Minister Vosooghoddoleh secretly granted Great Britain direct authority over transportation, financial, and military institutions in Persia. Great Britain had stopped paying oil royalties because Persia failed to protect British assets from attack by anti-British gangs and the occasional Soviet agent. The Persian government was almost completely without authority across Persia.

1920 AD

When word of the secret agreement with the British leaked out, rioting erupted in many areas, and anti-government forces began to organize. The incompetent and unpronounceable Prime Minister Vosooghoddoleh was forced to resign and was replaced by an equally powerless, but somewhat more pronounceable, Prime Minster Moshiroddoleh.

The government of Persia was weak and disorganized. A fast-riding, fierce tribe from the north, a.k.a. the Soviet communists, invaded northern Persia. The Soviets shelled Anzali for three days and then captured the city and set up a camp for the organization of a massive communist revolution in Persia.

The Islamic Persians were none too impressed with the offers to join an atheist revolution in exchange for free vodka, and the massive communist revolution failed to materialize at that time. The Persian government was up to its neck in poverty and internal strife and agreed to surrender its territory north of the Aras River to the Soviet Union. That area is modern day Turkmenistan.

1921 AD

A Persian military leader who distinguished himself in WWI, Reza Khan, seized power with the help of the British. He led the Persian Cossack Brigade in suppressing the many local uprisings across Persia.

1922 AD

Shia Islamic leader Sheik Abdul-Karim Haeri Yazdi founded a school for training Shia clerics in Qom. The hitherto insignificant Qom grew into the Persian center for religious and political discontent.

1923 AD

Reza Khan became the Prime Minister of Persia by unanimous election. There were only two votes in the election—his and the United Kingdom's. If he lacked legitimacy in democratic terms, he was at least intelligent and able to begin rebuilding and modernizing Persia.

1925 AD

The majority of religious leaders across Persia quietly formed an agreement to support Reza Khan because they strongly opposed democracy. In exchange, Reza Khan agreed to leave religious leaders in charge of many local civil matters. To the Islamic religious leaders, it seemed like a good idea and required no capital investment on their part.

1926 AD

Reza Khan ascended the Golden Peacock Throne of Persia and was crowned Reza Shah Pahlavi. His eldest son, Mohammad Reza, was declared the crown prince. Reza Shah intensified "Westernization" efforts. The religious leaders started to resent him, but they lacked the power to overthrow him. The Shah ordered the building of Persia's first cross-country railroad system, new schools, and industrial projects.

1935 AD

Reza Shah Pahlavi now felt strong enough to declare an official name change for the country from Persia to "Iran," which is the word that the common people of Persia have used to refer to themselves and to their empire since at least the time of Zoroaster.

Reza Shah began to resist British influence. He outlawed the use of the veil for women, and as his government became more effective, he regained control of local civil matters. When there was an uprising instigated by angry Shia Islamic leaders at the sacred Imam Reza shrine in Mashhad, Iran, Reza Shah ordered his military to crush the rebellion. Several hundred protestors were killed.

1941 AD

Reza Shah started to get cozy with Hitler and Mussolini. The British and Russians, uncomfortable with this growing bromance, moved in and saw that Reza Shah was deposed. To accomplish this, the Russians brought their message to bear in their usual fashion with kidnapping, blackmail, and brute force. As for the British, they were experienced hands in Asia and used not only troops, but also those age-old British political art forms commonly known as bribery and blackmail. The crown prince,

Mohammad Reza Shah Pahlavi, was placed on the Golden Peacock Throne.

———

L et's pause a moment and let that sink in. It is a popular political myth in the United States that "the" Shah of Iran came to power in 1953 when the United States pulled him out of thin air, "overthrew a democratically elected government," and placed him on the throne to be a US puppet dictator. As one can see, like most Sound Bite History, that was not quite the case. We will get to the events of 1953 in the next chapter.

———

6

RISE OF THE AYATOLLAHS

SEPTEMBER 2, 1945 AD

On the deck of the USS *Missouri* in Tokyo Harbor, General Douglas MacArthur, representing the Combined Allied Forces, accepted the surrender of Japanese General Yoshijiro Umezu and Japanese Rear Admiral Tadatoshi Tomioka. Thus ended WWII. Admiral Chester Nimitz signed on behalf of the United States of America. The War was so vast and hideous that between fifty-five and seventy million people died worldwide, and another fifteen million human beings remain forever unaccounted.

1946 AD

As a direct result of the political maps drawn up at the Potsdam Conference at the end of WWII by the United Kingdom, the United States, and the Soviet Union, both the Soviet Union and the United Kingdom officially departed from Iran. Note we said "officially." The Soviet Union pretended to leave, but the Soviets never did go home once they were invited to a party. They stayed in Iran in a clandestine capacity to continue fostering a communist rebellion.

The Potsdam Conference agreement did not require the United Kingdom to leave, but the United Kingdom choose to go voluntarily. Losses in blood and treasure through the forfeitures of some of its colonial holdings and the long dark night of WWII had left the United Kingdom struggling through extreme economic and social challenges. As a result, the United Kingdom had to withdraw from Iran and try to reinforce its more critical colonial holdings in India and Suez.

June 26, 1950 AD

Haj Ali Razmara became Prime Minister of Iran. Though he had attempted a better deal, he planned to sign a new agreement with a British oil company and the UK government that was less favorable to Iran than other agreements in force in Venezuela and Saudi Arabia. Razmara also planned on instituting more democratic reforms and granting local authority to locally-elected officials. This frightened the Shia religious leaders.

March 7, 1951 AD

A member of the Fadayan e Islam, a politically activist fundamentalist Shi'ite group, assassinated Prime Minister Razmara. The Shia religious leaders controlled the Fadayan e Islam, but no plot was tied to them.

With Razmara's demise, the Soviets found their window of opportunity. Their man, Nationalist Muhammad Mossadegh, became prime minister due to Russian election interference—the same Russian election interference that Russia has practiced around the globe on a regular basis since 1917.

Keeping with communist fashion and most likely Soviet direction, one of Mossadegh's first moves was to nationalize the oil industry. The United Kingdom declared an embargo on Iranian oil. A power struggle brewed between the Mohammad Reza Shah Pahlavi and Mossadegh.

August 16, 1953 AD

Mohammad Shah ordered Prime Minister Mossadegh to resign his office. Mossadegh, supported by a growing Soviet-backed communist movement, refused the order. At this point, the Soviets had undermined a great deal of the Shah's most reliable supporters with untimely accidents, blackmail threats, and bribes. It was no longer safe for the Shah and his family to remain in Iran. The Shah went into exile in Rome.

August 19, 1953 AD

Before the Shah and his entourage could finish unpacking, the CIA and MI-6 arranged a counter-coup against Mossadegh. Because of their fear of communism, the Shia mullahs quietly supported the counter-coup. General Fazlollah Zahedi was installed as prime minister.

The Shah tucked his toothbrush back in his bag and returned to Iran.

Some of Mossadegh's key supporters were imprisoned and tortured. Some were executed by firing squad. Mossadegh, himself, was kept under house arrest by the Shah's regime. Mossadegh died March 5, 1967, at age eighty-four in a hospital in Tehran. Bringing an entirely new level to house arrest, Mossadegh was denied a funeral and buried in his own living room.

We know what you're thinking. . . . What did that do to the property value? . . . We don't know, but if it's not on a Tehran Haunted House Tour, someone is missing a good bet.

1955 AD

The United Kingdom, Turkey, Iran, Iraq, and Pakistan signed the Baghdad Pact. The Pact granted the United Kingdom a leadership role in the region's fight against communism.

1957 AD

The CIA trained a secret police organization for the Shah named SAVAK. SAVAK answered directly to the Shah and not to the elected members of the Majlis.

1963 AD

Mohammad Reza Shah announced the White Revolution. The plan was to increase local democratic institutions, build more industry, complete land reforms, and lessen rural Iranians' dependency on the mullahs. The White Revolution also included voting rights and equal protection under the law for Iranian women.

The mullahs were incensed and did all they could to resist modernization. Ayatollah Khomeini was jailed for plotting against the government.

1964 AD

Khomeini was released from jail. He immediately attempted to organize a revolution against the government and against the modernization of Iran. He was exiled to Iraq, where he continued his work against the government of Iran.

1972 AD

US President Richard Nixon agreed to arm the Shah with the intention of preparing Iran to better resist threats by the Soviet Union. Iran purchased $4 billion USD in arms shipments.

1975 AD

Continued military expenditures and a drop in oil revenue caused economic problems in Iran. Khomeini's forty-nine-year-old son died, and the mullahs accused SAVAK of murdering him. Others suspected the Soviet KGB of the murder.

1978 AD

Mohammed Shah announced more modernization reforms. The mullahs were angered and organized more protests.Rioting broke out. The Iranian police killed several hundred protestors in Tabriz, Tehran, and Qom. Ayatollah Khomeini was exiled to Paris, where he did a great job playing the Western press. He managed to sell himself to them as a democratic reformer and a supporter of freedom.

With few exceptions, the Western press got it completely wrong about Khomeini. That mistake was soon evident, but the press largely refused to admit it at the time, and they still deny that they were ever wrong about the nature of the evil that took the reins of Iran.

January 16, 1979 AD

The Shah and his family fled Iran as the government collapsed. Thus ended thousands of years of Persian monarchies in Iran.

February 1, 1979 AD

Posing as a religious leader, political con man Ayatollah Khomeini returned to Iran with promises of new freedoms and democracy. He brought, instead, a new Dark Age of ignorance and oppression to Iran.

February 14, 1979 AD

The mullahs' thugs invaded the US Embassy in Tehran and took one hundred hostages. Two senior ministers of the secular Iranian government quickly negotiated their release, and the mullahs' henchmen withdrew.

April 1, 1979 AD

Happy April Fool's Day. The Ayatollah announced the Islamic Republic of Iran and declared himself "Supreme Leader." The people of Iran lost judicial protection. Politicians could only run for office if Khomeini approved of them. The Islamic Revolutionary Guard Corps, a.k.a. "Revolutionary Guards" or "IRGC," become the new enforcement arm of the Ayatollah.The Revolutionary Guards were new in the secret police business, and they used many SAVAK members to build their organization. Women lost their civil rights. The Ayatollah announced that the United States was the Great Satan and kicked off his "Great Satan" public relations campaign. He nationalized all foreign assets, and book burnings began. Witch hunts against non-Muslims became a new recreational pastime.

October 22, 1979 AD

US President Jimmy Carter finally and most reluctantly allowed the Shah and his family entrance to the United States for the Shah to receive cancer treatment in New York City. At this point, the Shah and his family had fled through four countries of exile since their departure from Iran in January.

November 4, 1979 AD

In retaliation, Khomeini's thugs invaded the US Embassy in Tehran and kidnapped fifty-two Americans, demanding that the Shah be sent back to Iran for prosecution. Many American reservists started reporting for duty voluntarily. They knew President Carter would likely order a mobilization and attack on Iran. The order never came.

7

US HOSTAGE CRISIS AND OPERATION EAGLE CLAW

1979 AD

Rather than attack Iran, President Carter authorized the Pentagon to order US Army Special Forces Delta Force, commanded by Colonel Charles "Chargin' Charlie" Beckwith, to plan and train for a hostage rescue mission known as Operation Eagle Claw.

Delta Intelligence Officer, Captain Wade "Ish" Ishimoto, began long hours working with multiple agencies outside of the Army to construct an accurate picture of the situation in the US Embassy. Ishimoto and Beckwith shared relaxing breaks together from their work by burning up ammo at the firing range. These guys didn't intend to miss. Given any chance, they wouldn't.

The CIA was willing and ready to implement a wide variety of operations against the Ayatollah, and American CIA members volunteered in droves for clandestine operations in Iran. President Carter approved little activity against Iran.

"Old Hands" and "Youngsters" alike were deeply frustrated by the White House's unwillingness to engage in Human Intelligence

("HUMINT") operations and covert action in Iran and other locations. However, the CIA and military intelligence agencies still gained some valuable HUMINT, and the US Navy Fifth Fleet in the Indian Ocean was reinforced.

November 20, 1979 AD

Iran released thirteen US hostages.

April 24, 1980 AD

Operation Eagle Claw commenced. Helicopters launched from the USS *Nimitz* for a low level, nighttime flight into Iran. It would be a long flight to "Desert One" where they would refuel with fuel brought in by a C-130. The pilots, flying below Iranian Air Defense at an altitude of one hundred feet, faced a heavy sand storm.

The helicopters and pilots were worn down from hours of flying through wind-blown sand. Two helicopters broke down on the flight to the refueling stop. After a third helicopter collided with a C-130 at the fueling stop, killing eight members of the mission, Delta was left with three helicopters. The agreed-upon minimum was six birds to reach Tehran. President Carter ordered that the mission be aborted.

Beckwith was in agony, but he accepted that there was no rational way to continue the mission. Delta and their accompanying Army Rangers withdrew from Iran. Out of the failed mission came an eventual major reorganization of US Special Forces teams with direct funding and permanent infrastructure for the support of their missions.

The continuation of the Iranian Hostage Crisis played a part in President Carter's defeat in his re-election bid. We should remember that, in spite of what other criticisms we might make of President Carter, he insisted on taking the full blame for the failure of Operation Eagle Claw. At other times, on other occasions, other, less honorable men and women in government have behaved very differently.

July 11, 1980 AD

One American Hostage was released.

September 22, 1980 AD

A slow, but reasonably savage tribe from the Northwest, a.k.a. the Iraqi Army, invaded Iran.

Iran had been organizing a Shia resistance against the Sunni minority Ba'ath government of Saddam Hussein in Iraq. The Iranians wanted Iraq's oil, but Iran was in economic chaos thanks to Khomeini and his undereducated, over-empowered mullahs. Saddam and the Ba'ath party wanted Iran and its oil, but the geographical obstacles were considerable. The mountains of northwestern Iran once again played a part in its defense.

The Iraqi Army, equipped with older, inferior Russian equipment, was unable to move fast enough, and Iran mustered an effective defense. A bloody stalemate ensued.

The Iranians announced that the "Hand of Allah" had stopped the Iraqi invasion. What more likely saved them was the involvement of the militarily-inadequate Iraqi dictator Saddam Hussein in the planning and conduct of the war.

June 1981 AD

In a wild and reckless move, Iranian President Abolhassan Banisadr dared to question the absolute authority of the Ayatollah. Khomeini tossed him from office. A defecting Iranian Air Force pilot smuggled Banisadr out of the country, and he fled to France. Banisadr's closest friends and supporters were executed. Banisadr remains under heavy guard in France today.

January 20, 1981 AD

President Reagan was inaugurated. Khomeini ordered the release of the remaining US hostages.

1982 AD

Iran founded and financed Hezbollah in Lebanon. Hezbollah is a radical Shia group dedicated to the destruction of Israel and the conversion of Lebanon to a Shia Islamic state.

1983 AD

Saddam's regime used chemical weapons against Iranian soldiers and civilians, as well as against Iraq's own Kurdish citizens.

October 23, 1983 AD

Iran used Hezbollah suicide bombers to attack the US Marine barracks in Lebanon. Two hundred, twenty American Marines, eighteen US sailors, three US Army soldiers, sixty French servicemen, and six civilians were killed in the attack.

It is now public information that the NSA intercepted the order issued from the Iranian government to their chief terrorist in Beirut to attack the Embassy. The NSA failed to pass on the information to the Pentagon or the White House in time to prevent the attack.

1985 AD

As the war with Iraq continued, the United States attempted to broker weapons deals with Iran in exchange for the release of kidnapped Americans. This became known as the Iran Contra Scandal. Profits from the sales—unseen by most, but not all, Congressmen—went to support anti-communist contras in Nicaragua and bordering nations. Americans in the jungles and occasionally in the air of Central America were fighting a war on a shoe string, but that's a tale for another day.

July 3, 1988 AD

The Ticonderoga class cruiser USS *Vincennes* shot down an Iranian Airliner with two hundred, ninety passengers and crew. The airliner deviated from the normal route and seemed to be descending toward the *Vincennes*. At that point in history, the crew of the *Vincennes* had no technological way of identifying the aircraft as an airliner full of passengers.

July 18, 1988 AD

Iran agreed to a United Nations ("UN") Peace Treaty ending the war between Iran and Iraq. Depending on who you ask, the war cost Iraq nearly four hundred thousand deaths, and cost Iran close to one million.

February 14, 1989 AD

In yet another of his many political blunders, the aging and never-rational Ayatollah Khomeini declared a fatwa against UK author Salman Rushdie for publishing *The Satanic Verses*. The fatwa meant that any Muslim could murder Rushdie and get extra virgins in heaven for doing so.

June 3 1989 AD

Khomeini finally did something useful for Iran and the Iranian people. He died. The actual date is disputed. Television cameras transmitted live scenes from his funeral. A mob of zealots tore open his coffin and ripped his body apart in attempts to obtain sacred relics from the dead mullah.

June 4, 1989 AD

President Khamenei was appointed as the new Supreme Religious Leader. Islamic clerics around the world were shocked by his selection. They claimed that his religious training was very limited, like the rest of his education. His main qualification for the job seemed to be that he was Khomeini's favorite "gopher" during his exile.

Over time, Khamenei would prove to be as incompetent as his critics claimed he was.

August 1989 AD

Ali Akbar Hashemi-Rafsanjani was sworn in as the new president of Iran the same day that constitutional reforms took effect which eliminated the office of prime minister. Rafsanjani made slightly conciliatory remarks concerning the Great Satan. The United States released the last half billion of frozen Iranian assets from US banks.

June 21, 1990 AD

An earthquake in Iran killed forty thousand people. Seven hundred villages were destroyed. Five hundred thousand people were left homeless.

Iran remained neutral during the Iraqi invasion of Kuwait and during Operation Desert Storm, the allied invasion of Iraq.

1995 AD

The United States imposed economic sanctions on Iran for seeking to develop nuclear weapons.

8

NUCLEAR SHELL GAME

1995 AD

Intelligence agencies from various Western nations voiced concern that Iran had started a nuclear weapons program. The Western press said that Iran could build a bomb in five years. Western leaders were assured that a bomb would not be produced by Iran within ten years, based on where the Iranians were with resources and science. For most Western leaders, ten years was beyond their political shelf life.

The Israelis started whispering a little louder about the United States needing to lead a coalition against Iran to destroy its atomic energy facilities. The diplomacy game began.

1996 AD

China and Iran announced a joint project to build a uranium enrichment plant in Iran. Iran was feeling pretty cool about being big China's new little friend. China wanted the oil.

Within a couple of months, China had a mysterious change of heart and backed out of the program. We aren't sure who pulled which genie out of which cute little bottle, but we're glad they did. Somebody will tell Holmes the story when it's okay to tell him. In the meantime, the Secretary of State swore it was diplomacy that did it. She even might have believed that herself.

1997 AD

Iranian intelligence forces murdered four Iranian Kurdish refugees in Germany. Europeans didn't think it was funny. Educated people in Iran looked at the thousands of years of dues their ancestors paid on the long road to civilization, and they wondered why they were living under an idiot regime led by a fake cleric with enforcers made up primarily of Iran's least intelligent people, the Revolutionary Guards.

Ayatollah Khamenei started believing his own cooked statistics and mistakenly allowed moderate candidate Mohammad Khatami to run against his own hardline lackey that he was sure would win. Even with a little help from poll monitors in Tehran, Khatami, a.k.a. the intended sacrificial lamb, roasted the regime favorite in a lopsided election. It turned out that not many Iranians thought that the Dark Ages policies of the regime were all that funny.

The newly-elected President Mohammad Khatami still had to answer to the unelected Ayatollah Khamenei, so nobody was expecting Khatami to drag Iran very far back toward the twentieth century. Nevertheless, it was still a victory for hope and reason in Iran.

Khatami struggled against the dictator Ayatollah Khamenei and his goons, but he could not get much done for his country.

Hoseyn Ali Montazeri, an actual senior Iranian cleric with real training, publicly criticized Khamenei's dictatorial political power. He was placed under house arrest.

1998 AD

Iranian scientists were ordered to increase Iran's tunneling technology and skill in order to shield future underground nuclear facilities.

US intelligence services detected, tracked, and confirmed the launching of a medium range ballistic missile by Iran. The missile had the range to reach Israel.

Israel ordered its defense industry to step up efforts on missile countermeasures. The CIA reported to the US Senate Select Committee on Intelligence and the US president that Israel was now significantly less safe.

A few days later, the Secretary of Defense reported to Congress that Iran could build an intercontinental ballistic missile with the range to reach the United States within five years. North Korea needed oil and had been selling Chinese missile technology to Iran for oil and cash.

Iran's new radical pals in Afghanistan, the Taliban, cut the heads off eight Iranian diplomats and sent the heads to Iran in a box. Iran was not happy. They sent several army brigades to the Afghan border. Iran conducted overflights of Afghanistan. The threat didn't work. They were Taliban, not Pakistanis or Iraqis. They had no idea that they had suffered the indignity of being overflown by a hostile air force. Dignity had never really been a Taliban thing anyway.

1999 AD

The fun continued. Supreme Leader Khamenei's press controllers ordered the closing of a newspaper for being less than 100% devoted to the adoration of Khamenei. Students in Tehran were angered and they protested peacefully. Revolutionary Guard thugs disguised as angry civilians raided the student dormitory and beat and kidnapped students. Six days of escalating protests ensued. Over one thousand, two hundred students were arrested. Some of them were never heard from again.

2000 AD

Iran held elections for the Majlis. In spite of creative, Chicago-style election practices in Tehran, the reformers won an overwhelming majority. Once again, more pure and devout Iranians had demonstrated through their votes that their devotion to Allah did not extend to the Ayatollah Khamenei.

Iranian reformer Saeed Hajjarian became President Khatami's political adviser. The Revolutionary Guards suspected Hajjarian of releasing information to the press about the routine murders of moderates in Iran. Hajjarian was shot in the face on the steps of the city council, but he lived. Khamenei could not believe his bad luck.

2001 AD

Moderate Khatami won re-election. Khamenei asked his elections specialists what he was paying them for.

Holmes was sitting in a hotel room in Germany when he found out. Before long, he got a call from friends in the United States. They had a good laugh. They asked themselves what Khamenei was paying his election specialists for.

2002 AD

US President George Bush accused Iran of being a member of the Axis of Evil. The Western press fretted that Iran would become angry at us.

We know what you're thinking. . . . As compared to what?

The exiled Iranian National Council of Resistance reported to the Western press that Iran was building a secret underground nuclear facility at Natanz. President Bush and US allies had already been told.

2003 AD

Iranian Sunni leader Abdolmalek Rigi founded Jundullah to fight against the Iranian regime. Most folks assumed that the Saudis and their Gulf State Sunni pals were funding him. When IED bombs produced in Iran for use in Iraq started occasionally blowing up in Iran, Khamenei wondered what he was paying his bomb makers for. As for the Iranians that hated the regime that they lived under, they were not about to rally to the banner of Sunni-brand terrorists.

Students protested in Tehran again. The press coverage was more intense this time, and fewer students vanished into thin air. Protesting in Iran still takes great courage, as not all protestors survive.

Shirin Ebadi, a human rights activist, became Iran's first Nobel Peace Prize winner. She is a lawyer who had become Iran's first female judge in 1975, but she was fired after the 1979 revolution. Even with her family's many political connections, it's amazing that she survives. She now lives in London.

Forty thousand people were killed in an earthquake in southeast Iran.

Iran signed the Paris Agreement with European countries, purportedly agreeing to suspend uranium enrichment and allow more stringent inspections of its nuclear facilities.

2004 AD

A train crash in Iran killed about two hundred, sixty people. It may or may not have been an accident. It may or may not have been an act of sectarian terrorism.

Ayatollah Khamenei finally stopped believing his own propaganda. He accepted that most Iranians hated him and his thugs. He outlawed all candidates except his hand-picked lackeys. Finally, the conservatives managed to eke out a victory against themselves in the elections.

2005 AD

One ultra-conservative by the name of Mahmoud Ahmadinejad won the presidential election after all reasonable adults were removed from the ballot. This guy had run on the most ridiculous, obsequious, Khamenei-worship platform imaginable. You just know his mother wasted that money she paid for those acting classes.

9

NUCLEAR CHICKEN

AUGUST 2005 AD

After the election of ultra-conservative hand puppet Mahmoud Ahmadinejad as President of Iran, his boss, the Supreme Leader Ayatollah Khamenei, ordered the International Atomic Energy Agency ("IAEA") seals at the Isfahan nuclear site to be broken. The seals had been installed as part of an economic agreement with the European community.

Europe responded by quietly attempting to get Iran to adhere to the agreement that it pretended to agree to in 2003.

January 2006 AD

Iran broke the IAEA seals at the Natanz uranium enrichment facility. Muhammad al Baradei, the Director General of the IAEA, was concerned and showed it publicly. US President George W. Bush announced that the United States would not accept uranium enrichment by Iran.

He failed to mention what "non-acceptance" would consist of beyond frowns and condemnations.

April 2006 AD

Ahmadinejad proudly announced that Iran had enriched uranium to 3.5% concentration. This level of uranium was concerning, but not anything like the approximately 90% that is needed for a uranium fission weapon. Ahmadinejad understood this, and he knew the United States wouldn't go to war for 3.5% uranium. However, he hoped to show that he defied the United States and the West. His minority of supporters in Iran cheered. The majority of Iranians were not thrilled by the news.

July 31, 2006 AD

UN Security Council Resolution 1696 demanded that Iran stop enriching uranium. Russia and China both cooperated with the resolution because both of those countries were trying to sell Iran reactor-grade enriched uranium at high prices. The resolution proved to be as effective as most UN resolutions, as in not at all.

December 2006 AD

The Iranian regime hosted an international conference for Holocaust denial. Ahmadinejad pretended to think that Western allies invented the Jewish Holocaust after WWII. Iranian apologists in the West later pretended that Ahmadinejad never said the many hateful things that he frequently said. More than anything, the "conference" showed how ignorant Iran's Ayatollah Khamenei is about how people outside of Iran think.

Iran's Holocaust denial scheme backfired on Iran. The UN passed a previously-stalled resolution blocking all vendors from selling Iran any nuclear equipment and technology that could be used in the development of a nuclear weapon.

February 2007 AD

The IAEA said Iran ignored yet another deadline for ceasing its uranium enrichment and called for more economic sanctions.

Hand puppet Ahmadinejad screamed more of his usual nonsensical denouncements against the evil Western world and the Zionists. Everyone wished he would get a new speech writer.

March 2007 AD

Operating on the principal that one can never have enough enemies in one lifetime, Iran kidnapped fifteen British sailors from international waters near its coast. The United Kingdom protested. Iran thumbed its nose. A few of the UK's least intelligent journalists questioned how "this disaster could occur."

May 2007 AD

The IAEA announced that Iran could develop a nuclear weapon within three to eight years if left unchecked in its efforts.

June 2007 AD

Riots broke out in Iran over gasoline rationing. It occurred to Iranians that it takes a truly talented and gifted government to produce a gasoline shortage in a petroleum-exporting nation. The various embargoes had some impact. Iran couldn't manage its oil industry well without outside help.

October 2007 AD

The United States came to its senses and finally cut off the Iranian Revolutionary Guards and their many lucrative corporations from US banks. The White House admitted what lots of folks had known for a long time, which was that Iran was financing, training, and controlling the most active and best-armed insurgents in Iraq. Big surprise. Not.

February 2008 AD

Iran launched a test missile and said it was for scientific research. . . . Yes. That particular branch of science is called, "Hitting Europe and Israel with nuclear weapons."

March 2008 AD

Ahmadinejad visited Iraq for a rousing round of denouncements of Zionists and the West. Everyone outside of his Shia radical supporters in Iraq and Iran yawned.

After disqualifying all of the opposition from running for office, the "conservatives" won another round of uncontested elections in Iran.

In Iran "conservative" means, "I will lick the boots of Ayatollah Khamenei."

May 2008 AD

The IAEA announced that Iran was still withholding information about its atomic programs. Holmes was in Washington that day. He and his friends chuckled about the "shocking" news.

November 2008 AD

Ahmadinejad congratulated Barack Obama for winning the US presidential elections. Obama cringed.

December 2008 AD

The Iranian police state raided the office of the human rights coalition led by Nobel Peace Prize winner, Shirin Ebadi. Iran said the office was acting as an illegal organization.

March of 2009 AD

Iran's support for US President Obama ran out. Iran accused him of being another Zionist. Obama was relieved by the denounce-ment. Back then, being liked by Iran was even more damaging to an American politician's reputation than being liked by Fidel Castro.

We can only assume the White House considered it a good day PR-wise.

April 2009 AD

Iranian-American journalist Roxana Saberi was convicted of spying for the United States by an Iranian court. She was sentenced to eight years in prison. That it was an eight year sentence rather than hanging was clear proof that the Iranians knew she was not spying.

May 2009 AD

The US State Department announced that Iran was the world's leading terrorist supporter. The folks over at CIA shrugged. Many employees remembered to be grateful they didn't work for the State Department and didn't have to talk to the press.

Iran freed Roxana Saberi and she returned to the United States. We're not sure who got it done. We're glad they did.

June 2009 AD

Mahmoud Ahmadinejad defeated a popular opposition leader and former Iranian prime minister named Mir-Hossein Mousavi in a rigged presidential election. Protests erupted across Iran. Mousavi was hardly a reformer, but he wasn't Ahmadinejad, so the public supported him beyond what the regime had calculated they would. Khamenei ordered crackdowns against the protestors.

After the murder of a female protester named Neda Agha-Soltan was filmed on a cell phone and posted on YouTube, cell service was interrupted in Iran. Approximately one hundred protesters were believed to have been murdered by Khamenei's goons. Hospitals reported over a thousand seriously wounded.

The international press caught on to what teenagers with cell phones had been aware of for over a week and started covering the protests as well as they could. Several foreign journalists suffered beatings, arrest, and banishment from Iran. Several

Iranian journalists and journalism students who covered the protests vanished.

August 2009 AD

Ayatollah Khamenei got tired of Ahmadinejad pretending to be a real president and humiliated him by publicly demanding that he dismiss some of his key appointees. Ahmadinejad was filmed pouting.

Khamenei announced that he decided the "opposition candidate" and his top supporters were not actually foreign agents. . . . Brilliant.

September 2009 AD

Iran stopped denying that it was building another uranium enrichment plant at Qom, Iran. The IAEA was angry, and it only took them two months to formulate a statement denouncing the Qom uranium plant.

The denouncement was so effective that Iran announced it would build ten more uranium enrichment plants. Given that they were already operating one thousand, three hundred uranium processing centrifuges, ten more plants would be eleven more plants than they could possibly need for running nuclear reactors for generations of electricity.

December 2009 AD

The death of the one-time Ayatollah Khomeini supporter-turned-dissident, Grand Ayatollah Hoseyn Ali Montazeri, triggered a new wave of protests in Iran. About twelve people were murdered or vanished. Montazeri was once considered Khomeini's natural successor, but he had broken with Khomeini because of the mass murder of opposition members in Iran and because of Khomeini's insistence on absolute authority.

January 2010 AD

Nuclear physicist Masoud Ali-Mohammadi was murdered in Tehran. The regime blamed the killing on Israel and the United States, saying it was an attempt to damage Iran's nuclear program. However, Ali-Mohammadi was not important to Iran's nuclear program. He likely was murdered for openly supporting opposition candidate Mir-Hossein Mousavi and for refusing to step back into line. He had told his students not to fear death when considering protest because death can only hurt for a few seconds, but that the regime had hurt Iran for decades.

Iran stepped up missile production. The United States announced that US Patriot Air Defense Missiles would be deployed to Bahrain and other parts of the Persian Gulf to defend against possible missile attacks.

February 2010 AD

Iran announced that it was "willing to ship its uranium overseas for conversion to fuel rods for peaceful use in Iran." The offer was welcomed, but not followed by action. Russia had been offering the service to Iran for years. Nobody took Iran too seriously in its announcement. In any event, the process did not prevent Iran from continuing to enrich uranium beyond the levels needed for fuel rods.

June 2010 AD

The UN imposed its fourth set of economic sanctions against Iran. Iran responded with its standard anti-American/anti-West/anti-Zionist dogma.

July 2010 AD

The international community condemned Iran for condemning Sakineh Ashtiani to death for "adultery." Iran changed its mind about stoning her for adultery. Instead, it stoned her to death for an imaginary murder plot.

This sort of thing happens frequently in Iran, along with the public execution of juveniles who are accused of homosexuality. Few cases make it to the attention of the international community so when they do, some people are shocked. The condemnation means nothing to the police state that runs Iran under the guise of a theocracy.

September 2010 AD

Someone in the Bushehr Nuclear Facility forgot to not open porn on their work computer, and the system was infected with the Suxtnet Worm. The infection spread to other Iranian nuclear facilities. The press said it could have been a "nation state" that did it. . . . Yeah. Maybe so.

December 2010 AD

Switzerland hosted international talks with Iran. It proudly announced that a diplomatic breakthrough had occurred. The breakthrough? They had agreed to hold more talks at some date in the future.

February 2011 AD

Protests started up again in Iran.

Iran was an old hand at dealing with protests by this time. It had and still has a regular "protest response crisis team." The team beat a few hundred protestors bloody and killed a few more, and the others went home.

Iran sent one war ship and a support ship through the Suez Canal to Syria. This was the first time that an Iranian war ship had transited the Suez since the mullahs came to power in Iran in 1979.

April 2011 AD

In the dark comic opera that we call Iran, the rebellious actor Ahmadinejad again made the mistake of pretending to be a grown up president, and again Khamenei publicly humiliated him by flexing his "supreme authority muscles." Remember, Ahmadinejad ran on a sycophantic political platform of "anyone who suggests disagreement with the Supreme Leader must be stoned to death . . . twice." The Iranian president's restrained temper tantrums were rather hilarious to observe. Most Iranians found it the only thing about him that was funny at all.

September 2011 AD

Iran announced that the Bushehr Nuclear Power plant was on the grid. It was the first Middle Eastern nuclear power plant to go on line. The plant was originally a joint project between Iran and the United States during the reign of the Shah. The funny thing was that if Khomeini had not forced Iran back into his personal Dark Age in 1979, the plant would have been on line around 1985.

October 2011 AD

The United States foiled a plot by Iranian intelligence forces to assassinate the Saudi Ambassador to the United States. Iran denied responsibility.

November 2011 AD

An unexplained explosion occurred at an Iranian Missile Development Center. A Revolutionary Guards general was killed.

The IAEA announced that it had irrefutable evidence that Iran was attempting to build a trigger for a nuclear weapon. The United States, Canada, and the United Kingdom increased financial sanctions against Iran and froze Iranian assets. The European community did not follow suit.

In its state of financial crisis, the European Union ("EU") could not ignore Iranian oil. The first Iranian missile could fall on Paris someday, but in the meantime, Paris could not survive without the oil. The United States and Canada could promise the United Kingdom that it would reopen wells and keep the United Kingdom supplied, but it could not promise to do so for all of Europe.

Apparently concerned that not everyone on the planet was completely despising his regime, the Ayatollah Khamenei's thugs attacked the British Embassy in Tehran. Some of the younger thugs wanted to attack the US Embassy, as well. The old timers had to remind them that the United States has no embassy in Iran. The average person in Iran wondered why in the name of Allah, after thousands of years of seeking to refine a civilization, they must endure such madness.

December 2011 AD

European intelligence services anguished over the increase in uranium refinement in Iran. Iran had the missiles. Successive Western politicians had put the day off for "tomorrow" for a long time. Tomorrows ran out. Faced with threats of yet more sanctions, Iran announced it would close the Persian Gulf to oil traffic. It didn't. Within the confines of White House instructions, the Pentagon tried to answer media questions about "what if."

January 2012 AD

The EU decided it couldn't wait any longer to act, and it announced an embargo against Iranian oil. Iran responded by claiming that it would destroy any US Navy vessels that attempted to transit the Strait of Hormuz. The US Navy sent another carrier into the Persian Gulf, which was joined by British and French war ships. Iran did not attack them.

The value of Iranian currency plummeted on world markets. Financial panic set in in Iran. The Iranian government froze the bank accounts of many Iranians.

Oil prices climbed. Our "friend" Saudi Arabia reduced oil production.

February 2012 AD

Iran denied IAEA inspectors access to the Parchin weapons development site south of Tehran. The Parchin site is where the United States and the United Kingdom believed Iran was attempting to construct an eight hundred-mile range missile for the delivery of nuclear warheads.

The United States and Israel openly held joint meetings. The United States started issuing more direct statements concerning possible joint strikes by the United States and Israel. At that point, the only substantial, unsettled question between Israel and the United States was what would trigger any strikes against Iran.

The White House was told that within two months, Iran could build a nuclear weapon. During the last week of February, doors in the Capitol started opening, and people started talking across the aisle. The political chatter decreased. Congressmen were looking more serious and less theatrical. One could say they were even starting to look like a "government."

Welcome to the fight, people.

10

IT'S OKAY TO LIE TO INFIDELS

FEBRUARY 29, 2012 AD

The Pentagon entertained the press openly. It announced that it was determined to stop Iran's nuclear weapons program. When the press asked if the United States had the capability to destroy Iran's deep underground uranium enrichment facilities at Natanz and Fordo, the Pentagon stated that it could destroy these sites with large, conventional weapons.

Short of a substantial strike, nothing would dissuade Supreme Leader Khamenei from seeking nuclear weapons. Holmes's best guess was that Khamenei was not convinced that Obama would make that strike, and especially not before the 2012 election. Khamenei was right.

March 2012 AD

UN inspectors announced that traces of uranium enriched at 27% were found at Iran's Fordo nuclear site. Europe, Canada, and the United States held talks with Iran about its nuclear program. Iran continued to stall, and the talks proved to be as useless as the last hundred or so attempts at diplomacy with the Iranian government.

March 2 – May 4, 2012 AD

Iranian President Ahmadinejad, getting testy and wanting more money and power, ran his own anti-Western/anti-reason supporters against Ayatollah Khamenei's anti-Western/anti-reason supporters in parliamentary elections. Not surprisingly, the Ayatollah's supporters won. No one else did.

Approximately 60% of Iranians were in neither of those two extremist camps, but their opinions and votes didn't matter because no serious challengers were allowed to run in the elections.

June 2012 AD

The United States exempted India, Malaysia, South Africa, South Korea, Sri Lanka, Taiwan, and Turkey from any economic penalties for continued trade with Iran in exchange for those countries agreeing to cut oil imports from Iran. The original deal was that no one could import any oil. These countries wanted to violate the embargo, so the United States negotiated this reduction in consumption of Iranian oil.

July 2012 AD

The EU boycott of Iranian oil took effect. The Iranian economy took yet another turn for the worse. Social unrest increased. The IRGC and other supporters of the regime beat and arrested unarmed protestors.

An unarmed majority cannot influence a well-armed minority, and a well-armed minority rules Iran. If the pen is, indeed, mightier than the sword, freedom of speech must be instituted in Iran before reason can conquer ignorance and brutality in that country.

July 8, 2012 AD

While suppressing a Shia protest in Saudi Arabia, the Saudi police shot and wounded the Iranian-backed Shia cleric Nimr al-Nimr. The Saudis then jailed the cleric. Iran protested al-Nimr's arrest and complained that Shias are treated poorly in Saudi Arabia. The Iranians did not explain why Shias are treated poorly in Iran.

September 2012 AD

The IAEA announced that Iran doubled its production capacity at the Fordo uranium enrichment facility. It also significantly hampered another IAEA attempt to inspect the Parchin military site. Canada broke off diplomatic relations with Iran due to Iran's nuclear program and Iran's continued support for the Assad regime in Syria.

October 2012 AD

Iran's currency hit a record low against the US dollar. The Iranian Rial had lost 80% of its value since 2011, in part because of international sanctions and in part because of waning public confidence in Iran. Black market currency trading was increasing in that country.

The EU announced more economic sanctions against Iran. The Iranian regime ordered that more riot police and political thugs be kept on alert, but it made no policy changes to alleviate the stress on the Iranian people.

Ahmadinejad's mouthpieces claimed Iran had achieved a uranium enrichment concentration of 83%. They needed better than 90% concentration for reliable and powerful fission weapons. The Iranian government continued to stall the West as it attempted to produce such weapons in the form of nuclear warheads and nuclear armed missiles. The West continued to make that easy for Iran by procrastinating in taking any effective action.

Clandestine operations had thus far prevented the Iranian regime from adequately refining uranium to the high concentration necessary for the assembly of a nuclear warhead. This success was helped by the fact that not all of Iran's scientists and members of government agreed with the regime's desire to create a nuclear arsenal. Low cost, "low kinetic" operations against Iran were attractive because of the low political risks to Western governments that such operations presented, but such operations could not prevent the assembly of a nuclear weapon indefinitely.

The Iranian regime had been consistent and predictable in its foreign policy and military objectives since the 1979 founding of the Islamic Republic.

June 15, 2013 AD

Hassan Rouhani won Iran's presidential election. Rouhani was presented as a "reformer." However, if he had not already quietly committed his obedience to Ayatollah Khamenei, it is unlikely that he would have been allowed to run for office. Rouhani claimed that he was going to institute broad civil rights in Iran. It never happened.

Rouhani's selection by Khamenei and his Supreme Council of the Cultural Revolution was a wise one from their point of view. Rouhani was well informed about the world outside Iran, and his public relations and diplomatic skills were quite refined. He would do a much better job of deceiving Western nations.

November 23, 2013 AD

The White House announced that it had just finalized the 2013 Geneva Accord, an "interim" agreement with Iran concerning its nuclear program. Given that other Geneva Accords had been concluded, and subsequently disregarded, it is useful to specify the "2013" aspect of *that* Geneva Accord. After the announcement of *that* Accord, constant news chatter flooded the airways about what it meant, who it impacted, and whether it should be celebrated or cursed. The answers to those questions depended on who was talking.

According to the White House and staunch Democratic Party supporters, the 2013 Accord was a historic foreign policy victory. No surprise. But not all Democrats agreed. Democratic Representative Chuck Schumer said, "As for additional sanctions, the disproportionality of this agreement makes it more likely that Democrats and Republicans will join together and pass *additional* sanctions when we return in December. I intend to discuss that possibility with my colleagues." (Emphasis is author's.)

If we asked traditional Democratic Party detractors, the 2013 Geneva Accord was nothing more than appeasement. They said it was reminiscent of British Prime Minister Neville Chamberlain's Munich Accord with Adolf Hitler, and may result in Armageddon. No surprise.

According to Israeli Prime Minister Benjamin Netanyahu, the 2013 Accord was an "historic mistake." He said, "What was achieved last night in Geneva is not a historic agreement, it is a historic mistake. For the first time, the leading nations in the world agreed to the enrichment of uranium in Iran by ignoring the decisions of the [UN] Security Council that they themselves led." Some Israeli cabinet members condemned the Accord in even harsher terms.

Statements by the EU were largely supportive of the 2013 Accord as an important first step. However, France expressed disappointment with it. The French delegation to the negotiations in Geneva said, "We want to avoid the euphoria of the glass half full." They pointed out that in 2003-2004, Iran agreed to a similar suspension of uranium enrichment, but it never followed up its promise with action.

China and Russia were also both parties to the negotiations with Iran in Geneva. They both responded with diplomatic statements indicating that the Geneva Accord was a valuable first step in dealing with Iran's nuclear program.

The Kingdom of Saudi Arabia, a.k.a. America's favorite gas station, was outspoken in its criticism of the 2013 Geneva Accord and of the process that led to it. The Saudis were unusually blunt in their criticism of the Obama administration's entire foreign policy toward Iran, and they claimed that they were repeatedly lied to by the Obama administration during the negotiations with Iran. The Saudis went so far as to clarify that their foreign policy toward Iran would be conducted more independently, and that the Saudis would no longer follow the US lead or allow the United States to speak for them in any dealings with Iran.

In an unusual move, the Saudis engaged openly with Israel and discussed possible cooperation against Iran. The Sunni clerics that so heavily influence Saudi policy were routinely rabidly opposed to Israel. Either they had been momentarily brought to heel, or they were far more concerned about threats from Iran than they were about the existence of Israel. The Shia mullahs of Iran make no secret of the fact that they are committed to making Iran the sole Islamic Caliphate on the planet.

In Holmes's judgement, another possible consequence to Saudi Arabia's negative response to the 2013 Accord was that the Saudis may have felt free to negotiate with Pakistan to purchase nuclear weapons. Up to that point, Saudi Arabia had relied on the United States and the West to prevent Iran from obtaining nuclear weapons. That basic trust caused the Saudis to forgo the decision to acquire nuclear weapons of their own. They hinted that they were losing confidence in the West's ability and willingness to keep nuclear weapons out of the hands of the Shia mullahs in Iran, which could cause the Saudis to reconsider their decision.

So what, precisely, *was* the 2013 Geneva Accord? That, too, depended on whom you asked. According to the language of the agreement, Iran promised "cross my heart and hope to die" that its nuclear program would be solely for peaceful purposes. In return, the six other signing countries—the United States, the United Kingdom, France, Germany, Russia, and the People's Republic of China—agreed to see that UN Security Council sanctions would be lifted, along with multilateral and national sanctions related to Iran's nuclear program. A Joint Commission of the signing countries was to be established to work with the IAEA to facilitate resolution of concerns. Everyone agreed that the 2013 Accord was a "first step" agreement that would last six months while all parties formulated a more longterm, comprehensive deal. However, the reality outside of the language on the paper was a bit less clear.

According to the Obama administration and the European Union, the 2013 Geneva Accord slightly reduced Western economic sanctions against Iran in exchange for limiting Iran's ability to enrich uranium. By its terms, Iran was to keep concentrations of uranium isotope U-235 below 5%, which is useless for weapons except for "dirty bombs." It required Iran to scrap half of its stockpiles of uranium enriched at 20% or more, and to halt the construction of a heavy water reactor capable of producing plutonium. Iran was to allow daily inspections by the IAEA to verify compliance. The Obama administration said that the subsequent longterm agreement to be drawn up in the next six months would last "around twenty years." Originally, White House officials expected that the 2013 Geneva Accord would be in effect as of November 24, 2013.

If we asked Iran what the 2013 Geneva Accord meant, they would have told us that it meant Iran could still enrich uranium as it saw fit, and that *all* economic sanctions against Iran had been lifted. The Iranians were stating that the 2013 Geneva Accord would not take effect until January of 2014. Right after the Accord was supposedly agreed to in Geneva by all seven parties, Iranian President Hassan Rouhani told the Iranian media, "Let anyone make his own reading, but this right is clearly stated in the text of the agreement that Iran can continue its enrichment, *and I announce to our people that our enrichment activities will continue as before.*" (Emphasis is author's.)

Whatever the folks in the White House, 10 Downing Street, the Elysée Palace, the Kremlin, Beijing, or the Western media thought, claimed to think, or pretended to think that the 2013 Geneva Accord meant, it would have been in everyone's best interest if all parties to the Accord had actually agreed on what they were agreeing to do or agreeing not to do. At that point, the parties to the agreement, in particular the Iranians, did not seem to be agreeing to the same "Accord" that all other parties to the agreement indicated that they were agreeing to. At that point, we had only the Geneva *discord* to analyze.

Herein lies a critical problem in dealing with Iran. Whatever an Iranian president agrees to with the West or with anyone else is subject to the approval of the (supposedly) religious junta that has the final say in Iran. That junta is *still* led by the old Ayatollah Khomeini's water boy and amateur zealot, Ayatollah Khamenei. Khamenei may be disdained by legitimate Shia scholars around the world and might be scorned by Sunnis and nearly anyone else that knows about him, but he has the obedience of the Revolutionary Guards and the courts of Iran, so he matters.

Western European businessmen were quick to sign deals with Iran to sell it expensive technology and to purchase Iranian oil and gas. Those businessmen might have been surprised when they found out that Beijing and Putin Bahk (Bank Putin) were busy secretly negotiating "capitalist pig" type post-sanction deals with Iran while the West was busy worrying about U-235 stockpiles. Western free market democratic type "capitalist pigs" had to move fast to beat out filthy communist dog type "capitalist pigs" in reaping any financial benefits from any reduction in the economic sanctions against Iran.

As is often the case, the devil is in the details, and neither the devil, nor the details, had yet played out.

December 9, 2013 AD

Engineer and former defense contractor employee Mozaffar Khazaee, a.k.a. Arash Kazaie, was arrested at Newark Liberty International Airport in New Jersey and charged with trying to ship highly-classified military documents to Tehran, Iran. According to court filings, the documents in question included technical manuals, specification sheets, blue prints, and other materials related to jet engines and to the US Air Force's F-35 Joint Strike Fighter. Khazaee is a native of Iran who became a naturalized US citizen in 1991.

The intercepted documents would have been immensely important to the Iranian government. One of Iran's major military goals for the previous thirty years has been to build an industry that could produce a modern fighter aircraft capable of standing up to American and European fighters. The documents that Khazaee was attempting to deliver to Iran would have helped Iran tremendously in achieving that goal. It also would have helped Iran to better formulate countermeasures against any F-35s deployed against them.

11

THE IRAN DEAL

July **14, 2015** AD

President Obama announced the "key parameters of a Joint Comprehensive Plan of Action" in Vienna. The Joint Comprehensive Plan of Action ("JCPOA") became known as the "Iran Deal." The Iran Deal purported once again to limit Iran's nuclear capabilities to peaceful pursuits and to allow for the lifting of sanctions against that country. Most importantly to Iran, the Iran Deal freed up tens of billions of dollars in oil revenue and frozen assets.

President Barack Obama, Secretary of State John Kerry, and representatives from the United Kingdom, France, Germany, Russia, and the People's Republic of China described the agreement with Iran as being a major historic breakthrough in relations. Supporters of the agreement described it as a historic triumph. Detractors were certain that it was an historic mistake. At the time, it was difficult to say how good or bad it would be for any of the concerned nations.

President Obama and his supporters presented the agreement as an alternative to war with Iran. Framing it in those terms made any agreement seem more palatable, but that ignored the various other options, including the status quo.

We should not forget that while the sanctions were in place, they helped prevent Iran from testing a nuclear warhead. It was clear that Iran had acutely felt the impact of the sanctions. Both keeping the sanctions in place or increasing them were viable options. At the time, White House spokesman Josh Earnest said that other options including increased sanctions were under consideration. Clearly the "we better sign it to prevent war with Iran" theory was salesmanship, and like most sales teams, the White House knew not to take its own marketing efforts too seriously.

If we compared the proposed terms of the JCPOA with past negotiation results, it appeared, from a US point of view, to be an improvement over previous Iranian positions. However, some of the more worrisome terms of the agreement included permitting Iran to retain illegally-built facilities at Fordow and Arak, allowing Iran to preserve its stockpiles of enriched uranium, and phasing out most restrictions on Iran's nuclear activities after ten years.

US Secretary of State John Kerry claimed that expecting Iran to close the aforementioned facilities and reduce its stockpiles of enriched uranium would have amounted to "Iranian capitulation," and, therefore, was not achievable.

It's worth noting that the entire reason for the sanctions during the previous fifteen years was to get Iran to capitulate on the point of nuclear weapons development. The United States and the West could have achieved Iranian "non-capitulation" without the previous fifteen years of negotiations and diplomatic breakdancing.

Other countries with skin in the game saw the Iran Deal from their own perspectives.

Israel sees itself as the future target of any Iranian nuclear weapons. Given that the Iranian leadership had so often labored to convince the world that they wished to annihilate Israel, it was easy to see how Israelis did not wish to place much stock in anything short of a completely enforceable, airtight nonproliferation agreement with Iran.

It might have been reasonable for the White House to assume that Israel would not accept any agreement with Iran. It might even have been reasonable for the White House to give up trying to placate the Israeli government. However, it was unwise for the White House to do so as openly and blatantly as it did. In Holmes's opinion, the administration should have at least publicly dealt with Israel with its usual politically-feasible feigned concern. After all, those were, in large measure, Israeli lives that the negotiators took to the poker table with Iran.

The Saudis and the Gulf States might not have any deep concerns for Israeli lives, but they have lived next to the Iranian theocracy long enough to worry about their own vulnerability to Iranian weapons development. The fact that Iran sends terrorists, advisors, missiles, and other weapons to the Houthi rebels in Yemen, along with Iranian power-grabbing efforts in Iraq, has further raised the level of distrust among Iran's Gulf neighbors.

And as for other overprivileged playboys . . . Let's not forget that the White House had to satisfy the collective wishes of the US Congress before the United States was officially a party to any treaty with Iran. The White House tried to disarm the US Congress by calling the agreement a "not-a-treaty." Congress bought into it and approved the JCPOA in September of 2015.

And the Iranians, themselves?

Alarmingly, the Iranians began backpedaling from the agreement even before they signed it. As with the 2013 Geneva Accord, Iran's interpretation of the terms of the JCPOA were vastly different than the interpretation the White House and UN Security Council described.

One glaring example was that the Iranian government said the agreement allowed them to keep ten thousand uranium enrichment centrifuges, while all other parties to the negotiations said that the agreement allowed for a little over five thousand centrifuges. Doubling the uranium enrichment capacity makes a huge difference in any nuclear weapons program. Yet at the same time the Iranian leadership was telling the world press that Iranian nuclear weapons programs were a figment of the US government's imagination, it was telling the Iranian people that they were not giving up their right to produce nuclear weapons.

In spite of the vaunted Iran Deal, Iran continued to give heavy support to internationally-identified terrorist groups while expanding its ballistic missile program.

For the actual text of the Joint Comprehensive Plan of Action, click here or go to https://www.documentcloud.org/documents/2165388-iran-deal-text.html.

12

DEAL, OR NO DEAL?

AUGUST 2015 AD

Iranian-controlled Shia activists in Saudi Arabia increased their protests against the Sunni-controlled Saudi Arabian government.

February 2015 AD

Ayatollah Khamenei belatedly spoke out against the continued beheading of Christians by ISIS terrorists. "We don't forget how much Iranian Christians have taken pains to render services, and some of them have martyred in Saddam's war against Iran." Khamenei advised Muslims to help Christians in need while he extolled that the Islamic Republic of Iran treats people of different faiths equally. He did not explain how Iran's new equal treatment of all religions works with the government's continued oppression of non-Shia Muslims or its goal of annihilating Israel.

September 10, 2015 AD

In a speech about Israel, Supreme Leader Khamenei clarified Iran's stance on religious freedom by announcing that "Israel will not exist in twenty-five years."

December 2015 AD

Iran repeatedly, publicly threatened that Saudi Arabia would "suffer severe consequences" if it proceeded with the execution of Saudi Shia cleric and protest leader Nimr al-Nimr.

January 2, 2016 AD

Saudi Arabia beheaded leading Shia cleric Nimr al-Nimr. Iran did not hide its fury and frustration. Iran's inability to prevent Nimr's execution was a major blow to its status amongst Muslim countries. Using one of Iran's favorite foreign policy tactics, the Iranian government allowed a mob in Teheran to set fire to the Saudi Arabian Embassy.

January 16, 2016 AD

The UN claimed that Iran had complied with nuclear facility inspection requirements as per the 2015 JCPOA, and the UN announced that international economic sanctions against Iran were lifted. However, not all UN inspectors agreed, as Iran continued to block inspection of key nuclear sites.

European nations, ever mindful of oil import costs, were anxious to increase trade with Iran. A few major European industrial giants were also anxious to sign large contacts with Iran.

January 25, 2016 AD

President Rouhani embarked on the first European state visit by an Iranian president since 2000.

November 8, 2016 AD

Donald Trump won the US presidential election. Part of his campaign platform included his intention to withdraw the United States from the Iran Deal, which had been supported by the Obama administration.

May 20, 2017 AD

With the candidates carefully controlled by Iran's Supreme Council, Hassan Rouhani was re-elected president.

June 7, 2017 AD

Seventeen people were killed and forty-three people were seriously injured in attacks on the Iranian Parliament and the shrine of Ayatollah Khomeini. ISIS claimed responsibility. The Iranian Revolutionary Guards claimed that US President Trump ordered ISIS to conduct the attacks. Given that President Trump had openly waged war against ISIS, it seemed highly unlikely that ISIS would follow orders from the United States.

December 2017 AD

Protests against the Iranian regime increased in several cities. President Rouhani and Supreme Leader Khamenei vacillated between announcing sympathy for the protestors and vowing to crush them. Rouhani and Khamenei went with crushing them.

May 8, 2018 AD

After Iran continued to block inspections at key nuclear sights in violation of the 2015 JCPOA, President Trump announced the US withdrawal from the Iran Deal. Iran responded by announcing that it would begin increasing its uranium enrichment capacity. It already had.

July 5, 2018 AD

Iranian president Khamenei threatened to disrupt the flow of oil through the Persian Gulf.

August 7, 2018 AD

The United States re-instituted some of the previously-cancelled economic sanctions against Iran.

September 22, 2018 AD

Jihadis opened fire on a military parade in Ahvaz, Iran, in the Khuzestan Province. At least twenty-five people were killed and seventy wounded, including women and children.

Khuzestan has a large non-Persian and non-Shia Arab population. It also has a great deal of oil. Sunni Arab nationalists and an ISIS group both claimed responsibility for the attack.

The Iranian government first blamed "the United States, Israel, and its regional allies" for the attack. Iran later decided that the United Kingdom, Denmark, and The Netherlands were responsible, because they supposedly harbored and assisted the attackers. Some Iranian government spokesmen claimed the Kurds did it. Finally, Supreme Leader Khamenei announced that it was, indeed, the fault of a US conspiracy.

November 5, 2018 AD

A second phase of US economic sanctions against Iran began.

March - April 2019 AD

Already weak from years of sanctions, the Iranian economy suffered more damage when heavy rains in some regions of Iran caused serious flooding, resulting in widespread damage and the deaths of about seventy-five people.

April 8, 2019 AD

US President Trump designated the Iranian Revolutionary Guards Corps as a terrorist group.

April 15, 2019 AD

The United States imposed economic and travel sanctions against IRGC leaders. The IRGC announced that strikes against the United States and its allies in the region would increase. They did.

May 5, 2019 AD

US National Security Advisor John Bolton announced that the United States was sending a carrier strike group and Air Force bombers to the Middle East in response to increased threats by Iran and its surrogates in the region. Bolton stated "The United States is not seeking war with the Iranian regime, but we are fully prepared to respond to any attack, whether by proxy, the Islamic Revolutionary Guard Corps, or regular Iranian forces."

May 8, 2019 AD

Iran announced that it would increase its uranium enrichment operations. It already had.

May 12, 2019 AD

Four commercial ships were sabotaged off the coast of Fujairah, United Arab Emirates ("UAE"), including two Saudi Arabian oil tankers, one Norwegian oil tanker, and an Emirati bunkering ship. The UAE and everyone in the region other than Iran blamed Iran. Iran denied involvement.

May 14, 2019 AD

Iranian-backed Houthis used Iranian-supplied drones to attack and damage a Saudi oil pipeline that bypasses the Strait of Hormuz. Saudi Arabia and the United States blamed Iran. Iran denied involvement while it simultaneously issued more threats to block the flow of oil from the region.

May 19, 2019 AD

A rocket fired by Iranian-backed rebels in Iraq landed near the US Embassy in Baghdad. No one was injured. President Trump tweeted, "If Iran wants to fight, that will be the official end of Iran. Never threaten the United States again!"

June 12, 2019 AD

Japanese Prime Minister Shinzo Abe arrived in Tehran in a bid to mediate between the United States and Iran. The following day, he met with Iran's Supreme Leader Khamenei.

Khamenei refused to negotiate with Abe.

June 13, 2019 AD

As Japan's Prime Minister Abe was attempting to engage Khamenei in peace negotiations, terrorists attacked a Japanese tanker and a Norwegian tanker in the Gulf of Oman. The Iranians vacillated between knowing nothing about the attacks and claiming that they were on the scene and had rescued crew members from the oil tankers that they supposedly knew nothing about.

The US Fifth Fleet said it received two separate distress calls from the tankers in a "reported attack."

June 17, 2019 AD

The US Pentagon announced that it was sending an additional one thousand troops to the Middle East in response to Iran's increasing terror activities.

June 20, 2019 AD

Iran shot down a US drone operating in international air space. Some hawks in the West called for massive military retaliation against Iran.

In Holmes's opinion, since no US or allied personnel were harmed by the Iranian attack against the drone, that would have been an overreaction.

June 21, 2019 AD

US President Trump announced that he had authorized, but then called back, a strike against Iran in order to prevent casualties to hundreds of Iranian civilians. The aborted attack might have been conducted as a test of Iran's response to an air attack and as an attempt to jolt the Iranian leadership out of its false sense of security. It seemed to work. Though the Iranians felt obliged to increase their drum beating, the oil tanker attacks were halted.

June 25, 2019 AD

President Trump ordered increased economic sanctions against Iranian Supreme Leader Khamenei and his closest associates.

June 28, 2019 AD

President Trump announced that Western allies and other nations that rely on the flow of petroleum and natural gas through the Strait of Hormuz should take responsibility for the defense of their ships. Trump clarified that the United States, which does not rely on Gulf oil exports, would provide intelligence and assistance, but not bear the defense burden alone.

Trump supporters cheered the announcement. Trump detractors were outraged and claimed that the policy shift to requiring US allies to contribute to their own defense will alienate those allies.

Germany announced that it would not participate in any US-led efforts in the Gulf, but it declined to make any efforts on its own. Given the decrepit state of the German Navy, the German government's decisions concerning the Gulf will have little practical impact on the situation.

June 29, 2019 AD

The US Air Force announced that it will deploy F-22 stealth fighters to the Middle East region.

July 1, 2019 AD

Iran announced that it had exceeded the cap on uranium enrichment to which it had agreed. The following day, Iran announced that it had not violated any agreements. The UN said it had.

July 4, 2019 AD

UK Royal Marines, customs agents, and police boarded and seized the Iranian supertanker *Grace 1* in waters off Gibraltar. The tanker was suspected of carrying Iranian crude oil to Syria in breach of EU sanctions.

July 8, 2019 AD

Iran again confirmed that it had surpassed the previously-agreed-to limits on uranium enrichment.

July 19, 2019 AD

In a move that somehow seemed to surprise the UK government, the IRGC seized a British oil tanker in the Strait of Hormuz.

July 25, 2019 AD

The UK belatedly announced that the Royal Navy will escort all UK vessels through the Strait of Hormuz. After decades of cuts in ships, sailors, and aircraft, the UK Royal Navy may well find itself challenged to defend UK commerce in the Persian Gulf.

August 15, 2019 AD

Gibraltar's Supreme Court ruled that the *Grace 1* must be released.

August 30, 2019 AD

The United States claimed that Iran was continuing to enrich more uranium and to higher concentrations than the agreements allows. Iran denied that claim.

Then, thumbing its nose once more, the Iranian government announced that it *was* enriching more uranium than was allowed by its agreements with the West, and to higher concentrations than it did, but didn't, but did, agree to.

13

FULLY PREPARED TO RESPOND

SEPTEMBER 4, 2019 AD

The United States increased sanctions on Iran and blacklisted an oil-shipping network controlled by the IRGC. President Trump said that the United States would not accommodate a proposal by France to throw a financial lifeline to Tehran. France seemed unconcerned by Iran's increasing nuclear activities.

September 10, 2019 AD

US President Trump announced that he had fired National Security Advisor John Bolton because he felt that Bolton was pursuing policies that were "too hawkish."

September 14, 2019 AD

Iranian-controlled Houthi rebels in Yemen attacked and damaged an Aramco oil depot in Saudi Arabia.

September 24, 2019 AD

President Trump addressed the UN in New York. He declared that Iran was the world's single greatest sponsor of terrorism and asked the UN to take action against Iran. The UN did what it almost always does, which is nothing.

November 2019 AD

Iran announced domestic fuel price hikes. This prompted mass protests nationwide. The Iranian government announced sympathy for the protestors, then decided the protestors are "agents of Western conspirators." Iranian police murdered over two hundred peaceful protestors, according to Iranian medical responders.

January 2, 2020 AD

Infamous terrorist Quds Force commander Qasem Soleimani was killed in a US drone strike at Baghdad Airport, prompting Iranian threats of retaliation.

Soleimani commanded terrorist groups in Iraq, Syria, Lebanon, and, to a lesser extent, in other areas. He repeatedly bragged about the murders of Western military members and civilians by the various groups under his command.

Iraqi terrorist and Soleimani's top Iraqi adviser Jamal Jaafar Ibrahimi, a.k.a. Abu Mahdi al-Mohandes, was also killed in the strike. Ibrahimi is credited with being the founder and leader of the Kata'ib Hezbollah armed group, which operates in Iraq. He was also the de facto leader of the Popular Mobilization Forces ("PMF"), an umbrella group comprised mostly of Iranian-backed Shia armed groups.

Some Western media outlets and some politicians questioned the validity of the attack on Soleimani. Apparently unaware of the previous four decades of history, they worried that Soleimani's death would cause the Iranian government to dislike the United States and the West. To no one's surprise who had studied history, Iran vowed revenge.

January 3, 2020 AD

Iran announced that Soleimani's deputy for more than two decades, Esmail Qaani, would replace Soleimani as IRGC Quds Force commander. Qaani was known to be less of a publicity hound than Soleimani was. We expected that he would bring a nearly-seamless management command change to the Quds Force with no significant policy or tactical changes. Any changes in the IRGC would, as they always have, come from the Ayatollah Khameini.

January 4, 2020 AD

Two small rockets hit the Balad Air Base near Baghdad. Two mortar rounds hit Baghdad's Green Zone. No casualties or significant damages were caused. It was believed that Iranian-backed Shia militia conducted the attacks.

January 6, 2020 AD

Iran announced it would no longer abide by any restrictions on its nuclear program. In other words, business as usual.

January 7, 2020 AD

Iran announced that during Soleimani's burial in Kerman, Iran "as many as twenty people" were stampeded to death. Kuwaiti Journalists in attendance claimed that at least fifty-six people died in the stampede.

The Iranian government claimed that over a million people attended the funeral. Iranian protestors claimed that the government used North Korean funeral protocols by bussing in thousands of Iranians who were forced to attend the funeral and threatened with arrest if they did not appear to grieve.

Iran launched twenty-two surface-to-surface missiles from Iran, targeting two Iraqi-US air bases. Fifteen of the missiles made it out of Iran and entered Iraqi air space. Ten missiles hit Ayn al Assad Air Base in central Iraq. One helicopter was destroyed, and buildings and a second helicopter were damaged. No US, Iraqi, or Allied personnel were killed. Eleven US soldiers were treated for concussions.

Worse casualties were avoided because most of the personnel had been moved to bunkers prior to the attacks, thanks to warnings that came first from US intelligence reports and later from Iraq. Some troops remained outside the underground bunkers at guard posts, prepared to repulse any follow-on ground attack by Iranian-controlled militias.

One missile aimed at the US- and Iraqi-controlled Erbil Air Base in northern Iraq fell short, and another hit the base but didn't explode. Some speculated that Iran notified Iraq of the attack in the hope of avoiding casualties because the Iranian government did not want to trigger more attacks by the United States. The speculation was plausible.

The Iranian government needed a show of force to demonstrate to Iranian audiences that they remained powerful and relevant, and that the United States was paying for killing Soleimani and his cohorts. With worsening economic issues and increasing protests across Iran, the Ayatollah and his pals could not afford to look vulnerable. Iranian media sources broadcast claims of "over eighty Americans killed" in the missile attacks.

An Iranian Air Defense installation shot down a Ukrainian airliner minutes after it took off from Teheran's Imam Khomeini Airport. One hundred, seventy-six people were killed.

January 8, 2020 AD

The Iranian government claimed the airliner crashed due to an engine failure and that rumors that it had been shot down by an Iranian Air Defense missile were absurd. They announced that the flight recorders had been recovered, and that they would not be turned over to Boeing, the manufacturer of the airplane.

January 9, 2020 AD

The Iranian government announced that claims that Iranian missiles shot down the Ukrainian airliner were part of a propaganda plot by the United States and its Zionist allies.

January 10, 2020 AD

The Iranian government announced that an Iranian Air Defense installation accidentally shot down the Ukrainian airliner.

January 11, 2020 AD

The IRGC planted a fake Pentagon memo showing that 139 service members were killed in the missile strikes on the two air bases. Many social media users took the bait and passed on the story.

January 14, 2020 AD

The United Kingdom, France, and Germany invoked a dispute mechanism in the JCPOA, charging that Iran had breached several key parts of the agreement. Some speculated that this move was in response to President Trump suggesting that the United States might place a 25% tariff on European vehicles.

January 16, 2020 AD

In the ongoing proxy war in Yemen between Saudi Arabia and Iran, the Iranian-backed Houthis used Iranian-supplied missiles and drones to attack a Yemeni government military base in Marib. Sixty people were killed and dozens more were wounded.

On Iranian TV, President Hassan Rouhani announced that he wanted to avoid war, and that the Iranian government was working every day for peace in the region. Rouhani did not explain how the day's missile attacks in Yemen fit into Iran's supposed peace plan.

Note: The Houthis are usually described as being Shia, but they are not actually all Shia. For the moment, they are a political organization rather than a religious organization. Their roots go back to more of a pan-Muslim beginning, and they accept both Sunni and Shia jihadis into their ranks.

January 20, 2020 AD

Iran Foreign Minister Mohammad Javad Zarif claimed that Soleimani's funeral marked the "end of the US presence in the region." It likely did not.

Commander of the Islamic Revolutionary Guard Corps Aerospace Force Brigadier Amir Ali Hajizadeh explained that the Islamic Republic's reprisal after the assassination of Lieutenant General Soleimani "will not be limited to firing a dozen missiles." In what is perhaps a wise PR move, Hajizadeh then shifted responsibility for avenging Soleimani's death to Allah. Militant Iranians who wanted more revenge against the United States did not need to be be patient with Hajizadeh and his command or with the Iranian government, but rather they needed to be patient with Allah.

22 January 2020

South Korea announced that it would divert a naval ship on pirate patrol off the coast of Somalia to the Strait of Hormuz area to join the US efforts to protect shipping in the area.

In what appeared to be a serious crisis of faith, Iranian Minister of Parliament Ahmad Hamzeh was apparently already impatient with the strategy of waiting for Allah to avenge the assassination of Soleimani. He offered a $3,000,000 USD reward for the killing of US President Donald Trump.

IN CONCLUSION

THERE IS PRESENTLY NO IMMINENT CONCLUSION TO THE IRANIAN theocracy's war against its neighbors, the United States, and its own citizens. Clearly, the Iranian government feels a critical need to bolster its image as a dangerous, ruthless, and unpredictable source of trouble in its neighborhood.

Though the Iranian government wishes to keep its many enemies and opponents guessing about what it might do next, its primary goals won't change unless a new revolution occurs in Iran. Which US politician resides in the US White House or which UK politician resides at 10 Downing street won't be particularly relevant.

Seven successive US presidents have tried their hand at diplomacy with Iran, and the results have not varied much. The United States has attempted everything from threats to bribes to neutralize the Iranian threat, but to no avail. The United Kingdom has tried its own diplomatic initiatives with the same poor results.

The goals of the Iranian theocracy have remained the same since its 1979 rise to power.

Its first goal is to remain in control of Iran. Toward that end, the mullahs will continue to brutally crush any domestic threats to their power.

The theocracy's second goal is to increase its influence and power throughout the Middle East and the world. For the moment, the United States, the United Kingdom, and other Western nations are in no immediate danger of becoming Shi'ite theocracies. Unfortunately, the West does remain vulnerable to Iranian-sponsored terrorist acts.

Iranian government officials at times deny this, but they never go very long without reminding us of their desire to hurt the United States and other Western nations. Even though those threats are often followed hours later by claims that Iran seeks peace, the threats must be taken seriously. The fact that Iran continues to work toward building nuclear weapons and longer-range ballistic missiles is clear evidence of the Iranian government's hope of becoming a bigger threat to the West and its neighbors. Iran's attacks on oil tankers in the Persian Gulf and the Gulf of Oman are another clear manifestation of its unwavering intentions toward the West and toward its own neighbors in the region.

Locally, Iran has repeatedly stated that it opposes the existence of the state of Israel, and on multiple occasions, Iran has said that it will, indeed, annihilate Israel. Iran also continues to seek the installation of a Shi'ite theocracy in Iraq, and it works toward that goal by financing and controlling various Shi'ite militia and terrorist gangs in Iraq, Syria, and Lebanon.

Iran will keep reminding the West that if we make the Iranian government mad, it might decide to annihilate us all. It won't. Iran has little to gain and an entire country to lose by starting a full-scale war with the United States. Even the Iranian mullahs can figure out that one.

Chicken Little would undoubtedly tell us that a war between the West and Iran would lead to World War III and a nuclear Armageddon. It won't.

Russia's Putin and China's Ping will claim to believe Chicken Little. They don't. Neither of them is going to start a nuclear war in defense of their beloved friends in Iran for one simple reason. They don't have any beloved friends in Iran. Those two barely have anything like "friends" within their own respective countries, much less in any others.

The United States and Western nations, in general, have two essential questions to ponder concerning Iran. The first and most important question is, "Will the West allow Iran to develop nuclear weapons?" Western governments have been consistent and unanimous in answering the question with a "No." The second question is just as critical, but less simple. "What will Western nations do to prevent Iran from obtaining nuclear weapons?"

Experience tells us that most Western nations will stick to frowning faces, expressions of disappointment, and mild finger-wagging-type responses while hoping that the United States and possibly the United Kingdom will deal with it while they sit back and criticize the United States and/or the United Kingdom for dealing with it. That won't change.

The wild cards in dealing with Iran are Saudi Arabia and its Arabian neighbors, as well as Israel. Saudi Arabia and the Gulf states have the most to lose in the Iranian Armageddon bingo game because they live next door to Iran. They have all been increasing their air defense capabilities as well as their air forces.

Israel has stated that it will not allow Iran to obtain nuclear weapons. *When* Israel would act and *how* it would act to prevent that remains to be seen. In Iraq and Syria, Israel moved early to oppose nuclear weapons development. Iran is now much further along in its nuclear weapons program than either Syria or Iraq ever were. Iran has multiple nuclear facilities, and several of them are in deep underground complexes. A single air strike against a single target would not be enough to halt Iran's progress toward nuclear weapons.

Iran's goals are consistent. The United States and its Western allies, such as they are, need to decide what they will do to prevent Iran from obtaining nuclear weapons. Thus far, the strategy has been to rely on diplomacy and sanctions. While the sanctions have badly damaged the Iranian economy, the Iranian government has not been forced to halt its development of longer-range missiles and nuclear weapons. The United States and the United Kingdom would do well to recognize and accept the lack of support from their other "allies" and not waste time explaining their actions.

The lessons of North Korea's success in developing nuclear weapons should not be forgotten. Buck passing and *mañana* tactics won't work. The United States and the United Kingdom should instead do their best to coordinate with Israel and the Gulf states in preparing a viable plan for halting any nuclear weapons development in Iran while effectively opposing Iran's attempts at Shi'ite revolutions in Iraq, Lebanon, and Yemen.

Thus far, UK Prime Minister Boris Johnson and US President Donald Trump have shown a willingness to join ranks against the Iranian junta. In dealing with Israel, they have both discretely moved toward developing a more united front against Iran.

As always, based on the philosophy that what is good for the West is bad for them, Russia and China will employ their usual propaganda efforts against any US and UK efforts in the Middle East. Therefore, the United States and the United Kingdom need to conduct quiet negotiations and consultations with the Gulf states and Israel. Loud, open negotiations with big PR efforts might appease some segments of the public in their respective countries, but they would also give China and Russia a solid target to loudly oppose in every way possible. Trump and Johnson can continue to tweet about other things to their hearts' content, but they need to keep their cards for the Iranian game close to their chests.

To be clear, the United States is not in conflict with the Iranian people—that rich, sophisticated society that was Persian long before it was co-opted by an Islamic fundamentalist theocratic regime. We share the same enemy with the people of Iran, the majority of whom oppose the junta that oppresses them and denies their will. We have sympathy for the Iranians who are exiled from their homeland because they would challenge the theocracy that stripped them of their rights. We have the deepest respect for the Iranian people who dare to challenge their theocratic oppressors, and who join in the protests not knowing if they will be arrested, beaten, tortured, or killed by their own government in their quest for freedom.

The Iranian people deserve better. They deserve a government that serves their best interests first—not the interests of the mullahs, not the interests of domestic or foreign oligarchs, and not the interests of China, Russia, or *any* other country that would pillage Iran's oil while caring nothing for its people. The Iranian fight for freedom may take a month, or it may take decades. We don't know, but we believe that in the end, the people of Persia will prevail.

PHOTO GALLERY

Visit our photo gallery with illustrations of some of the individuals and events referenced in this book at our website, BayardandHolmes.com.

———

KEY FIGURES IN ESPIONAGE
THE GOOD, THE BAD, & THE BOOTY

WITH THE VOICE OF FORTY-FIVE YEARS IN THE INTELLIGENCE Community, Bayard & Holmes explore the lives of the espionage elite.

- A one-legged woman operating behind Nazi lines, deemed to be "the most dangerous spy in all of France."
- A young man left for dead, not worth a Viet Cong bullet, who survives to fight terrorists for six more decades.
- A homeless child who becomes an iconic showgirl, entertaining world leaders while running spy rings from the top stages of Europe.
- A traitor operating at the top of Western intelligence whose betrayals caused the deaths of thousands.

More heroic and more treacherous than any fiction Hollywood could produce are these genuine operatives of the Shadow World, who prove that "we're only human" is not an excuse to fail, but a reason to succeed.

Available at BayardandHolmes.com/nonfiction.

ACKNOWLEDGMENTS

Our deepest gratitude . . .

To Vicki Hinze, publishing angel and dear friend.

To Julee Schwartzburg, our editor. She didn't actually edit *this* book, but at this point, we would thank her if we were writing a grocery list. She's just that good.

To our beloved spouses. To know us is to love us, but we're hard to get to know. Thank you for making the effort and sticking with us through this journey called Life.

To Jenny Hansen and S. Osito for cover design input.

To our beta readers, Dani Homados and Kerry Meacham.

To all of the dedicated professionals who gave us their time and efforts in the review and editing process.

And to our wonderful readers. You make our efforts worthwhile.

Thank you, one and all.

PRAISE FOR BAYARD & HOLMES

"When it comes to research into the clandestine depths of spycraft, the dynamic duo of Bayard & Holmes have put together a must-read Spycraft series that is written with authority, yet easily digestible. I've already added their books to my shelf of writing essentials—you should, too!"

— JAMES ROLLINS, #1 NEW YORK TIMES BESTSELLER OF
CRUCIBLE

———

"*Key Figures in Espionage* is a rollicking ride through some of history's most notorious espionage personalities. Well researched and written, the deep dive in to the Cambridge Five is particularly interesting. This book is great for not only the casual reader or spy fan but also for those who are more well versed in the subjects."

— DOUG PATTESON, FORMER CIA OPERATIONS OFFICER

Made in the USA
Middletown, DE
17 June 2022

67339215R00070